CLANE

the village we knew

CLANE

the village we knew

BRYAN SAMMON, PADDY BEHAN AND LIAM BURKE

NONSUCH

First published 2006

Nonsuch Publishing Limited
73 Lower Leeson Street
Dublin 2
Ireland
www.nonsuch-publishing.com

British Library Cataloguing in Publication Data.
A catalogue record for this book is available from the British Library.

ISBN 1 84588 537 6

Typesetting and origination by Tempus Publishing Limited
Printed in Great Britain

CONTENTS

*Dedicated to everyone included in this book
who enhanced and enriched our childhood*

Paddy Behan, Bryan Sammon and Liam Burke, the authors.

Clane village in the early fifties.

ACKNOWLEDGEMENTS

We wish to thank Mario Corrigan and all the staff in Newbridge Library, especially Carol Kiely, who did outstanding work; to Breeda Behan for her advice and mammoth work and who took on this project morning, noon and night in the last stages; to Seamus Cullen for his valuable guidance and inspiration; to all who contributed chapters to this book; to all who generously gave photos for the publication – Betty Brogan, Jack Dunne, Michael Richardson, Mary Timpson, Seán McManmon, Pat Harty, Pat Shortt, Kevin Mahony, Marie Coonan, Patti McCormack, Liam Armstrong, Billy McAndrew, Anthony Byrne, Lorraine and Brian (Clane Photo Centre), Margaret Woods-Corcoran, Christina McIntyre, Chrissie O'Toole, Tony McKenna, Bridget Behan, Maura Dunne, Molly Delaney, Carmel O'Hara, Pat Burke, Mary Dunne, Olive Dempsey, John Tierney, Murt Logan, the *Leinster Leader* and *The Irish Farmers' Journal*; Kathleen Delaney, Cait Cosgrove, Ann Heffernan, Lily Campbell, MaryJo Larkin, Lisa Kelly, Brige Cuddihy, Mary Healy, Joe Bracken, Larry Higgins, Jo Mahony, to our sponsors AIB Clane, Joe Mallon Motors, Dan and Marion Doolan (Londis Clane), Casey Trailers and Billy Smyth USA; Seán and Margaret Reilly. We also wish to thank our families, especially Imelda Ashe, the editor and staff of Nonsuch Ireland, and finally our wives Breeda, Maureen and Patti, for their patience and support throughout.

INTRODUCTION

It was not until 1989 that social history became part of the syllabus, to be examined for the first time in the Junior Certificate in 1992. Up to then, History studied important people and the major events of various centuries: the Roman Empire, the Norman invasion, the Reformation, the American War of Independence, Daniel O'Connell, 1916 to 1922, the founding of the UN and the EEC, and so on. But what of the lives of our great-grandparents? Their customs, fashions, leisure activities, commerce, and day-to-day living were neglected over the years.

Being the closest of friends from early childhood, we found in later life that we were not meeting so often, so we would promise to meet for a meal on each other's birthdays. During the meal (especially at dessert time) nostalgia would set in and memories come flooding back. We discussed characters, games, school, ways of living and shops with respectful fun and it struck us very forcibly that these memories would be lost in the years ahead. Encouraged by friends and contributors, we took up the challenge of setting our memories down in writing, and so *Clane: The Village We Knew* was born. While many of the people who feature in this book have passed away, to us they are very much alive, and their spirit lives on.

Paddy Behan
Liam Burke
Bryan Sammon

01 August 2006

THE HISTORY OF CLANE: EARLIEST TIMES TO 1945

Seamus Cullen

Clane is situated in the centre of North Kildare on the west bank of the river Liffey. The name is derived from the Irish word *Claonadh*, which translates as 'a sloping place'. This may refer to several sloping areas surrounding Clane, including the Main Street, which falls off steeply on both sides.

Prehistoric Period

Archaeological evidence shows that Clane has an ancient past, with human activity dating from the fourth millennium BC. This came to light following the discovery of a Stone Age fragment during excavations on the Sallins road close to the stream. The discovery of pit burials in Loughbollard confirmed that there was continued human presence in Clane in the Bronze Age.

THE FORD AT CLANE

Clane was a significant site in prehistoric times due to an ancient ford on the river Liffey: the principal road linking Nás Na Ríogh – the seat of the Kingdom of Leinster – and Tara – the seat of the High Kings of Ireland – crossed the Liffey at Clane. Military activity between the High Kings and the Kings of Leinster very often occurred close to the ford at Clane. One such encounter gave rise to the famous saga of King Mesgegra and his wife Queen Buan. According to the ancient legend, a famous duel between King Mesgegra and Conall Cernach, champion of Ulster, took place close to the Bullaun stone, which is situated at the stream, almost opposite the entrance into the Abbey Cemetery. Conall emerged victorious from the duel and beheaded Mesgegra on the Bullaun stone. Mesgegra was reportedly buried under the moate at Clane, and his wife Queen Buan, who died on seeing the severed head of her husband, was buried under the moate at Mainham.

Early Christian Period

Following the coming of Christianity around the year 520, St Ailbhe of Emly founded a monastery in Clane, on a site now identified as the burial ground surrounding the Community Centre. After the monastery was established, St Ailbhe decided to leave Clane and appointed St Sinchell, one of his followers, as the first abbot. St Ailbhe himself moved to Emly, where he died in 527. St Sinchell, having served for a period as abbot, moved to Killeigh, where he died in 549.

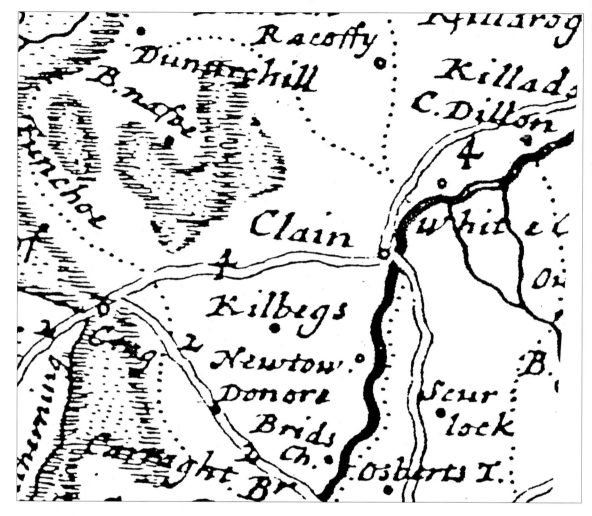

Molls Map *c.* 1720.

Opposite: Alexander Taylor's map of Kildare, 1783.

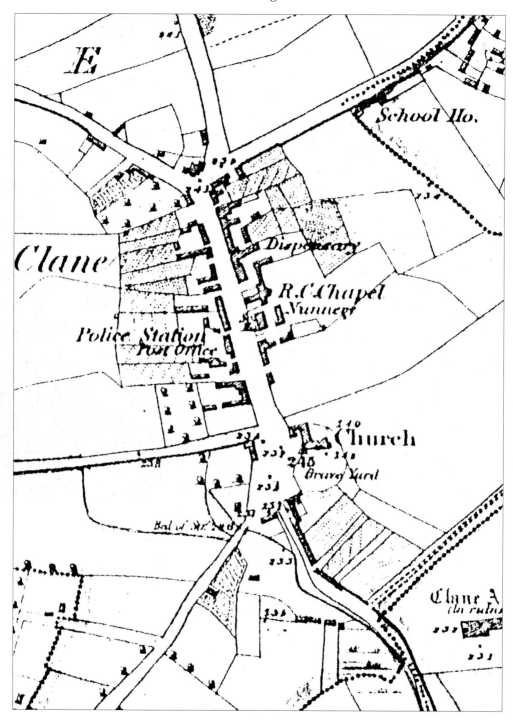

Ordnance Survey map of 1837.

Aerial shot of Clane, 1983.

Clane village in 1901.

Viking Plunder in 1035

In the period after St Ailbhe and St Sinchell, the monastery flourished and grew in importance as Christianity became dominant throughout the whole country. The monastery of Clane survived virtually intact during the period of the Viking raids in the ninth and tenth centuries. However, in 1035 the monastery was captured and plundered by a Viking raiding party from Dublin. The Vikings were pursued by an army led by the son of Donnchadh, son of Dómhnal, who eventually defeated them in a great slaughter.

Synod of 1162

The monastery of Clane soon recovered from the Viking raid and continued to grow and prosper throughout the eleventh and twelfth centuries. During this time, reforms aimed at bringing the Church in Ireland closer to the rules laid down by the Papacy were taking place, and a number of synods were convened for this purpose. In 1162, Archbishop Gelasius of Armagh convened a synod in the monastery of Clane. It was attended by twenty-six of the diocesan bishops, who were now introduced in place of the old tribal and monastic bishops. One of the bishops present was St Laurence O'Toole, Archbishop of Dublin, and many Abbots from leading monasteries also attended. The matter of the primacy of Armagh was debated, and the synod passed a decree that no one who had not graduated from the college of Armagh should be admitted as Professor of Divinity in Ireland. This firmly settled the unresolved issue of the Primacy of Armagh.

The Norman Conquest of Clane

At the time of the Norman Invasion, Clane was in the Celtic *tuatha* of Otomy, and this area was granted to Richard de Hereford. This Norman lord then created a barony in the old Celtic district of Otomy and centred it at Clane, where he established a manor. He enlarged the prehistoric Mesgegra Tumulus (the moat at Cois Abhainn) overlooking the ford, and remodelled it as a Norman motte with an adjoining bailey. A mill was then built close to the site of the present disused mill, and eventually the Norman settlement of Clane emerged.

The friary and abbey.

By the following century, the new Norman settlement of Clane had obtained borough status. The administration of the borough was in the hands of local officials known as the provost, bailiffs, and commonality of Clane. The provost was the leading official in the town and had a role similar to that of the present-day mayor.

A document issued by the King in 1391 granted the provost, bailiffs, and commonality of Clane the right to levy a tax on goods coming into the town for seven years in order to build a new bridge over the river Liffey. This bridge consisted of six arches and remained there until 1862, when it was demolished to make way for Alexandra Bridge.

Franciscan Friary

In the period following the Norman Invasion, many monasteries were replaced by friaries run by religious orders. In 1258, Gerald FitzMaurice FitzGerald, the fourth Baron of Offaly, founded a Franciscan friary in Clane. The site of this friary now corresponds to the Abbey Cemetery and some surrounding land.

Following Gerald FitzGerald's death in 1287, an effigy of his likeness was erected in the friary. It remained virtually intact on a marble monument up to the early 1700s. Today a fragment of the effigy survives.

In the year 1345 a general chapter of the Franciscans was held at the friary in Clane and in the following year a provincial chapter of the order was also held there. Accounts from 1433 indicate that an indulgence was granted as the friary was in need of repair. According to archaeological evidence, extensive repairs were carried out and new buildings were added at this time.

Reformation

Following the Reformation in the late 1530s, monasteries, friaries and abbeys were suppressed in areas held by the Crown and the friary of Clane was dissolved in 1540 and the lands confiscated by the Crown. Many of the buildings were demolished; one document from the period states that 'the Church, Chancel and part of the dormitory (of the Friary) were destroyed by order of the Lord Deputy for the purpose of repairing the castle of Maynooth'. In 1541 the lands of the friary were leased to many well-known members of the local nobility.

Clane in the 1640s

In 1642, during the Confederate Wars, Clongowes Wood Castle was attacked and captured by Crown forces. The victors executed the garrison and blew up the castle. Blackhall Castle was also badly damaged in a siege during the wars. In the aftermath of the conflict, a survey was carried out in 1654, which showed that two mills in Clane had also been destroyed, but four Castles within the town remained intact.

Emergence of Clane Catholic Parish

The parish of Clane up to the eighteenth century merely extended from Betaghstown in the north to Millicent in the south. Surviving records from 1731 show considerable alterations in parochial boundaries. Father Molloy, the parish priest in the Donadea area, succeeded Father Porter as pastor of Clane and Mainham. This created a new united parish. It is likely that Father Molloy had enjoyed the financial support of the Aylmer family of Donadea in the first decade of the eighteenth century. However, by 1731, this branch of the Aylmers had converted to the Established Church and Father Molloy had relocated to Clane. By 1738, Father Andrew Ennis was the parish priest of Clane and it is likely he gained the additional parish of Balraheen, which included Rathcoffey. This amalgamated parish survived unaltered until Staplestown/Cooleragh was formed in 1972.

Clane Mass House

In the period following the first decade of the eighteenth century, Mass houses were established in the Clane area. The first recorded Mass house in the locality was Rathcoffey chapel, which dates from 1710 and is still in existence. Separate Mass houses at Clane and Mainham date from 1715. Tradition suggests that there was a thatched chapel on the site of the Londis supermarket on Main Street in Clane, and this may be one of the Mass houses in question. The chapel at Mainham was located adjacent to Dunne's forge on 'Mainham Green'.

The 1798 Rebellion in Clane

The United Irishmen was founded in 1791, and two of the principal leaders throughout the early years of the movement had connections with Clane. Wolfe Tone owned a cottage in Blackhall, which he referred to in writings as 'Chateau Bou'. It was his principal residence before he was forced into exile in 1795. Archibald Hamilton Rowan, the best-known of the early United Irishmen leaders, lived with his family in Rathcoffey House until his arrest and eventual exile in 1794.

Another leading United Irishman in the area was Dr John Esmond, who also served as second in command of the local yeomanry, which was led by Richard Griffith of Millicent House. The rising was planned for the night between 23 and 24 May 1798. With Dr Esmond as the overall leader of Clane barony, the local rebels in the town elected James Tiernan, another serving member of the yeomanry, as their captain and leader of the local contingent. On the night of the rising, James Tiernan led the rebel attack on the town, but was beaten back with heavy losses. Richard Griffith arrived at this point, and took command. During the remainder of the night he beat back another rebel attack. By morning his superiors ordered him to abandon Clane and defend Naas, which was also under rebel attack at the time.

As he drew up his men in lines before moving out to Naas, other yeomen began joining the unit. One of them, Philip Mite, informed Griffith privately that his second in command, Dr Esmond, was secretly the rebel leader and had earlier been present during the attack on Prosperous. Seconds later, to the surprise of Griffith, Esmond arrived in uniform and reported for duty. Also reporting for duty that morning was James Tiernan, who had earlier led the Clane rebels. It appeared that neither of them was prepared to be publicly identified as a rebel, and that they were playing both sides. When the Clane garrison arrived in Naas, Griffith ordered the arrest of Esmond. He was not, however, aware of Tiernan's role in the rebellion. Tiernan, having witnessed the arrest of Esmond, deserted the yeomanry and rejoined the Clane rebels. Dr Esmond was later put on trial and eventually executed. The Clane rebels joined the North Kildare rebels and fled to the bogs around Timahoe, where they held out under the command of William Aylmer for three months, until favourable surrender terms were negotiated.

Clane in 1803

In 1803 a new conspiracy, led by Robert Emmet, conscripted an active group from Clane, headed by Matthew Donnellan, one of the wealthiest individuals in the town. Following the collapse of the Emmet conspiracy a number of men from Clane, including Donnellan, were arrested and briefly imprisoned. James Tiernan returned from exile and offered his services to Emmet. This offer was rejected but in the aftermath of the rising he was also arrested and imprisoned briefly.

New Parish Chapel

A new Catholic chapel was built in Clane by parish priest Father John Robinson in 1805. This building had a slated roof and was situated in the area between the entrance to the present parish church and Main Street. The building was described in *Lewis Topographical Survey of 1837* as 'a plain cruciform building in good repair'.

Clongowes Wood College

In 1813 General Michael Wogan Browne sold Castlebrown to the Jesuits, who established a college in the building. The Jesuits restored the original name of Clongowes Wood to the building and appointed Father Kenny as the first rector. The College opened in 1814 as a boarding school for boys, mainly from well-to-do Catholic families. It brought considerable benefits to the locality both commercially and in terms of employment.

Ministry of Father Kearney, Parish Priest from 1824 to 1842

Father Maurice Kearney was appointed parish priest of Clane in 1824. In order to supplement the income of the parish, Father Kearney decided to engage in cattle dealing and made substantial sums of money, which he used to finance parish building projects. He died in 1842 and was interred in the parish chapel. In his will he left in excess of £10,000, an enormous sum of money at that time. The bulk of the money, £8,000, was left to Carlow College, with substantial sums going to the chapels and schools of the parish, the Presentation Convent, and the poor of the parish.

Sisters of the Presentation Convent. 1839 – 2003.

The chapel and convent, Clane.

The Establishment of Presentation Convent

The Presentation Convent was founded in Clane in April 1839 by Mother Teresa Brennan. The new convent was built at the back of a school, which had been in use from 1831. The establishment of separate boys' and girls' primary schools also dates from this time. Initially there was a community of eight nuns, and in the years after their arrival a substantial advancement in education took place in the locality. It was to be the beginning of an era, which led to Clane becoming the hub of education in the general area.

New Church of Ireland at Millicent

In 1880 the Church of Ireland parishioners in Clane decided to vacate the old Protestant church and build a new one on a different site. Local landowner Thomas Cook-Trench presented a site for the new church on his lands at Millicent, and also contributed to funding the new building. Work began on the church in 1881 and was completed in 1883. It was designed by M.J. Fuller and dedicated to St Michael and All Angels.

New Catholic Church in Clane

In the early 1880s a new Catholic parish church was built in Clane, mainly through the efforts of parish priest Father Patrick Turner and his parishioners. The site chosen was at the back of the parish chapel, which was to be demolished when the new church was built. Preparation work on the site commenced in 1875, and the foundation stone was laid the following year. It was designed by Mr William Hague and cost £7,000 to build. There was a spiral included in the plans but unfortunately it was never built. The church was completed in 1884 and dedicated to St Patrick and St Bridget.

The GAA and Sport

In May 1885 a highly successful sports meeting took place in Clane, and this meeting evolved into the establishment of Clane Gaelic Football Club. The meeting also marked the beginning of the highly successful athletic career of local man Tommy Conneff, an early member of the club. During his outstanding career he broke several world records, including the four-mile world record, the world mile record (on two occasions) and the three-quarter-mile world record. The establishment of the Gaelic Football Club in Clane had a tremendous effect on society and life in general in the area. It also encouraged increased interest in the revival of nationalism that was taking place in the country at the time.

1916 to 1923 in Clane

Following the 1916 Rising there was an upsurge in support for the Irish Volunteers. In 1918, at an after-Mass meeting in Clane, the manifesto of the Irish Volunteers was read by Mick Sammon. Throughout the War of Independence, most of the young people in the Clane area were members of the IRA (the 'Old IRA'). There were two companies in the area: the local company in Clane was headed by Jack Greene and Fred Archer while the Mainham company was led by Pat Dunne. On 4 April 1920 the abandoned Royal Irish Constabulary barracks on Main Street was burned by the local IRA company. Later in the year there was a local connection with Bloody Sunday. On that tragic day, the inter-county football game was refereed by Mick Sammon from Clane, uncle of Bryan Sammon, one of the authors of this book.

Michael Sammon and his bride Elizabeth Gill.

Donadea Castle.

Following the departure of the British security forces, Clane suffered from what was described as 'a wave of crime and lawlessness'. It was not until September 1922 that the first gardaí took up duty in Clane under Sergeant James Finn. However, they had to contend with hostility from the anti-Treaty irregulars who were engaged in the Civil War. One serious incident between the unarmed gardaí and armed irregulars took place in March 1923, and resulted in the partial burning of the Garda Station. Apart from the sergeant, the other officers on duty on that occasion included Gardaí Lee, Coleman, O'Shea and Kennedy.

Clane Post-Independence

The new Irish government brought no overnight transformation in the fortunes of the area and throughout the 1920s Clane suffered from a severe recession. There were no factories or major centres of employment, and many young people seeking work were forced to leave the area. The only real employment in the locality throughout the period was in Clongowes Wood College. However, by 1929 the recession seemed to have abated, and the long road to recovery began, which would ultimately lead to a period of growth and to the prosperity now enjoyed by all in the community.

A view of the stream.

Connolly's bar in Newtonmoneenaluggagh, Ballagh Cross.

Firmount sanatorium.

Jim Malone's Barber Shop.

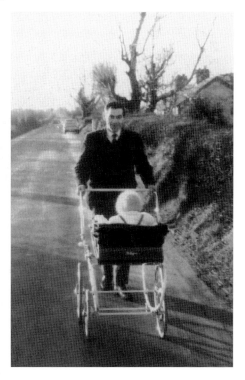

Matilda Jones, proprietor of the famous Jones' pub.

No cars, no potholes, only prams – John Tierney at Half-Mile Bridge

Taking a break – Dick Booth and David Gorry

Snagging turnips. John Tierney and Dave Gorry.

Paddy Casey at Jones'.

Lourdes, 1968.

Ned McCormack, trashing.

More stars of the future.

Pat Lynch's young charges.

Shoeing the horse.

Cocking the hay, Peter and Pat Shortt.

Horses and hay-making, in Richardstown

THEM WERE THE DAYS

Liam Burke

'AH, THEY WERE THE GOOD OLD DAYS.'

Many a time we have heard that statement, but when we were young we didn't realise they were the good old days. We would wake up on a freezing winter's morning, put on our clothes, if we could find them, get a basin and go outside to fill it from the icy barrel – no water mains – rush in, and wash ourselves with Sunlight soap. Meanwhile, our parents would be trying to boil the kettle on the primus stove and heat the thick porridge, which was cooked from the previous night. We had to go up to the pump at the top of the Terrace to fill a bucket with water, and carry it back to the house, spilling most of it. When it came to using the 'bathroom' it was again outside, and toilet paper was a luxury, used on special occasions or when our English relations visited us once a year – otherwise it was the *Independent* or *Press* that came to our rescue.

The wireless was turned on at 8a.m. when *Radio Éireann* opened with the news, and was followed until 9a.m. with sponsored programmes. Mícheál O'Hehir was on the Vaseline sports programme on Monday with all the results. *The Kennedys of Castleross* was a huge favourite, with Birdie O'Hanlon, the town gossip; Peader O'Mahony, the local farmer; and of course the dreaded arrival of Aunt Bridget and her son James. It was broadcast twice weekly for many years. Every Wednesday we listened to *Hospital Requests* and on Sundays we had *Living with Lynch*, *Question Time* and Din Joe with *Take the Floor*. Then Mícheál O'Hehir broadcast a football or hurling match. I remember the great excitement listening to the 1956 Leinster Final and to hear Des Marron's name mentioned. Other sponsored programmes were *Donnelly Sausages*, *Prescott's Cleaners and Dyers*, *Odlums* with Patricia O'Sullivan, *Gateaux Cakes*, and the very popular *Waltons*. My parents' favourite was *The Foley Family*. Radio Luxemburg was very popular on Sunday nights – Hughie Green presented *Double Your Money*, and there was also Michael Myles' show, *Take your Pick*. We always listened to *Top Twenty* from eleven to midnight, presented by Alan Freeman.

On Sunday evenings we listened to *The Sunday Play*, and I remember well the evening we first heard John B. Keane's *Sive*: the sound of the bodhrán, and the tinker's curse etc.

Ribbons – Ann Smyth, Breda Langan, Marie Dunne.

The Burke and Dunne clan, St Brigid's Terrace, Clane.

Party in St Brigid's Terrace. Back row: Brendan and Kathleen Mahony, Liam Burke, Francis Lehane, Marie Dunne, Margaret Donagher, Phil McCormack, Pat and Peter Burke. Middle row: Dessie Behan, Patricia Dunne, Carmel Donagher, Rita McCormack, Cora Mahony. Front row: Breda Dunne, Nellie Delaney, Claude McManmon, Declan Mahony, Kathleen Behan, Sheila and Ita Burke, David Mahony, Colm Behan.

The school around the corner; the convent school, First Class and Baby Infants, 1954. Back row: Barbera Gough, Eileen Noonan, Helen Keena, Helen Duffy, Rebecca Mahony, Breda Langan, Ann McGarr. Third row: Rita King, Ann Corrigan, Peggy McCormack, Rosaleen Shortt, Jacinta Connolly, Ann Smyth, Marie Dunne, Helen Stack, Kay Delaney. Second row: Marie O'Neill, Ann McEvoy, Cristian Reilly, Agnes Halligan, Mary Donnelly, John King, Norrie Stack, Gertie Connolly. Front row: Brendan Langan, Pat Burke, Tony Langan, Seán Farrell, Liam Burke, Frankie Behan, Dick Corrigan, Paddy Behan.

Old girls' school.

Our first classroom, convent school.

Everyone grew their own vegetables – including potatoes, cabbage, onions, beetroot, and lettuce – and rhubarb. We would borrow Kit McCormack's ass and cart to draw manure from Manzor's farmyard, and each time we went down McEvoy's hill, the ass would pull to the right at Aherns for his home on the Doctor's road, while I would pull the reins left for Manzor's, leaving us in the middle of the road. But not to worry – no traffic problems then.

Some boys started their schooling in the convent school, and I was one of them. We had Sister Brendan teaching us and I can't remember her ever being cross. She taught us from Baby Infants to First Class, and was fantastic, full of life. Sister Brendan played the piano, and one hymn we learned was 'Daily, Daily Sing to Mary'. Sister Anna taught us religion and I found she was not as friendly – she had her little pets, and one of those pets was Paddy Behan, who started school the same day as myself, and for over fifty years now we have remained the best of friends.

Back to the convent. I saw a flushed toilet for the first time, and was fascinated to see it working. Santa would come to visit us, and Sister Brendan made sure that we all got a present. When he was gone, Sister Anna would come into the class, disappointed that she had missed him. It was years later that I realised that she was *that* person.

Presentation Sisters, 1957. Back row: Patrick, Joseph, Columba, Margaret, Brendan. Front row: Brigid, Bertmans, Anna.

Little angels, where are they now? Sister Brendan and Mrs Peg Reilly, Mrs Maureen Coughlan and Miss Finn in the background.

The old boys' school.

Paddy, Seán Farrell, John King and myself made our First Holy Communion together, and Sister Anna brought the class to the church for rehearsal. She would give us the communion from a box, but the lads from the boys' school under Mrs Armstrong had to make do with ordinary white bread. There was very little communication between the two schools at that time. On First Holy Communion Day the four boys and fifteen girls had a big party in the classroom with our parents present. The boys' school, however, had no such privilege, don't ask me why.

We sadly bade farewell to the convent when we got older, and headed down the Dublin road to the boys' school, and what a difference: no smile of welcome from our teacher, Mrs Armstrong, just 'What's your name?' and 'Sit over there.' The playground was a bit of grass with plenty of mud. I eventually made my way down to see the 'flushed toilet' but was brought down to earth (pardon the pun) very quickly. No water, no towel, no flush – the 'toilet' consisted of five cubicles, and under each wooden seat was a drop of three feet to an open ditch. I can't remember ever 'performing' in those toilets. They were 'cleaned' every Friday between two and three by volunteers from higher classes, and the following is a true story:

Brendan Langan, who was always the life and soul of the class, and my brother Pat were on duty cleaning. They were in the ditch and heard one of the students coming into the toilet. The cubicle door closed, Brendan plucked a big thistle from the ditch and, as he was under the cubicle, stuck the thistle up. There was a huge roar, the door opened in haste, and the student returned to class, but remained standing for the rest of the class, and never reported the incident to the teacher.

Our co-author Paddy had chilblains on his hands and I remember the teacher holding his arm and hitting him on the knuckles with a pencil.

Jack and Dodo Delaney out for a stroll.

Ladies' choice: Statia Behan, Maura Dunne and Eileen Burke in Clane Hall, 1962.

When we progressed to fourth class we played football in the big field at the rear of the headmaster's house, but unfortunately we had no one to coach us, as the headmaster had no interest. We played our football in Manzor's GAA field after school and formed our own teams. Bryan, our co-author, played a huge part in organising the teams, and arranged a seven-a-side match with St Brigid's Terrace and Richardstown. The St Brigid's team were Thomas and Jim Mahony, Paddy and Frankie Behan, Seán McManmon, Bryan and myself, and Richardstown had a strong team with Mick, Willie and Pat Cooney, Billy Barrett, Joe Duffy, Pat Shortt and Billy Curran, with Joe Higgins and Joe Bracken also playing for them. The Terrace also played Philly McCormack, Pat Burke, Robbie Booth, Fergal Noonan and Simon Behan. We played against each other on several occasions over a four to five-year period, and some matches were very tough. I remember a fierce row broke out between Tom Mahony and Pat Shortt, which started in the field and ended up on the Capdoo road outside Mick Hanrahan's house. Meanwhile, Seán Farrell and Jim Byrne, two great friends from Loughanure, were interested in putting a team together to challenge the Terrace lads, and they roped in Brendan and Tony Langan, Dick Corrigan, Jackie Cooper and Joe Horan. We played them in Butterstream, where Clane Hospital now stands. We also played Blackhall, which included the great Kerryman Pat Griffin, Mick and Bill Cash, John King, Liam Higgins and Pat Corrigan. John Langan, brother of Brendan, also a great player, played for Blackhall, and the Terrace team objected because he was living on the Prosperous road. We were all around fourteen by now, and it eventually fizzled out, but we all remained friends and to this day recall the great rivalry.

We spent many sporting hours in Manzor's field, where, apart from football, Bryan organised athletics, and he himself excelled in the high jump and running. We would run a mile-race which was four laps of the field, and with over fifteen of us participating, Bryan would pull away from us with a half lap to go and win by over 30 yards.

Mrs Jo Mahony and John Delaney.

We also had a paper chase on various occasions, where two lads, who were called the hares, got a five-minute start on the rest of us. They would head off with two bags of newspaper, which were cut into small pieces, and as they went from field to field, would drop a few pieces of paper. On one occasion, Peter McManmon volunteered to be the hare and headed off up the College road with the bags of paper. We took off after counting the five minutes and headed towards Mainham, following the paper trail, turned left at the Gollymochy Bridge and headed to Harry Farrells, coming out at Jimmy Nestors and into Loughanure. Suddenly we were baffled – where did Peter go? Right? Left? After another thirty minutes of looking for paper we gave up and eventually headed back to Clane, where we spotted Peter, relaxing outside Lavin's shop, eating an ice-cream. 'Sorry about that lads, but I had to 'spend a penny' (not his exact words) in a ditch in Ballinagappagh and ran out of paper.'

We also played football in the Terrace, and many balls had to be retrieved from the front gardens that one of us would have kicked the ball into. Jim Mahony on one occasion kicked it into a lawn that was adorned with flowers and shrubs and, being a bashful lad, opened the gate, ran into the flowers and gathered the ball. This happened a number of times, and the owners, growing impatient, came out and warned us not to kick the ball in again. The match continued and the ball was kicked into the flowerbed again, and they came out and took the ball into the house. A minute later, we looked up to see black smoke coming out of the chimney.

In winter, when the weather was below freezing point, we would pour a few buckets of water on the road to make slides. One such slide was between our house and Mahony's, and it was about 30 feet long – we had endless fun for days, but Mrs Jo Mahony put a stop to it with a packet of salt, and told us to 'hook it'.

One winter's day, after a heavy night's snow, Jim Mahony, Paddy Behan and Pat Burke were coming home from the village when, on the approach to Phil McCormack's house, just before the entrance to the terrace, Phil Snr threw a big snowball at them. Jim and Paddy responded by hitting Phil, and after a few more snowball exchanges, with some snow going in through the front door, Phil warned them, but his words landed on deaf ears. Jim threw another, hitting Phil on the head, and that was that: Phil was not in the best of moods and jumped over the timber fence, taking after them. The boys started to run for home, and Pat slipped at Donagher's gate, but Phil was after the other two and ignored him. Jim was a good runner and Paddy had never beaten him in a race, but this time he passed Jim, doing a hundred miles per hour into Booth's garden, with Jim in pursuit. Phil was gaining ground and while Paddy made his escape over the gardens, Jim had only one option left: he burst in through Booth's back door and asked Mrs Booth, who was startled by the sudden entrance: 'Mammy wants to know what time it is.' Meanwhile, Phil was outside wondering where the lads had got to, and headed home.

McCormack's house has great memories for us; there was a big open fire with hooks hanging down, holding the kettle of water, and seats on both sides where we could see up the chimney. We played cards and Phil organised the 'Siege of Ennis', with him playing the mouth organ or the accordion.

In the summer there would be dancing out on the College road, and it would only be disturbed whenever the odd car arrived. Phil's favourite songs were 'I'm my own Grandpa' and 'Patsy McCann'. He had an old green Ford and brought us out to the Cott Bog where we loaded the lorry and filled his big shed with turf.

Christmas in the late fifties was a very special time, and the shops in Clane always decorated their windows with toys. Blake's had a very small window with a big bright star in the centre, while McKenna's had two windows with lights and toys of every description: lorries, dolls, prams, drafts, cowboy hats, holsters and cap guns. Lavin's would have a big stock of Christmas groceries and also a good selection of toys, and many hours were spent just looking into these windows.

I have fond memories of Christmas in our home and I continue to reminisce every year. My mother would make three puddings, including one for Emily O'Rourke, from whom we purchased our daily milk. All the ingredients went into a big bowl and as we stirred it, we would make a wish. Our postman, Christy McCormack, would be very busy for over a week before Christmas. We would receive cards from all our relatives, at home and abroad, and some would include a letter. It was the only contact, as we had no phone.

One Christmas, when I was around eight years old, my older sister, Moira, and I clubbed together to get a present for our parents. We had approximately 4s saved, so the two of us went down to McKenna's shop and bought perfume and a packet of hair clips for my mother, and a packet of cigarettes and a box of matches for my father. We went home and wrapped them, but Moira gave me the box of matches and hair clips while she proudly presented the more expensive presents. Christmas decorations, holly and balloons would be put up two days before Christmas. Every Christmas Eve, hail, rain or snow, our Uncle Paddy and Aunt Sheila cycled from Celbridge, which was eight miles away, and arrived in Clane at around seven, with bags full of goodies. As children we were excited about the arrival of Santa and anxious to get to bed and hang up our socks. The Clane Carol Singers would arrive singing 'Adeste Fideles' and 'Silent Night' and it would then be time to go to sleep.

My mother always cooked the ham on Christmas Eve, and after Midnight Mass she would have the ham sandwiches ready, as we would have had to abstain from food for five hours before the Mass. This was followed by a game of 25s, and at around 3a.m. on Christmas day, our aunt and uncle would head back to Celbridge on their bicycles. On Christmas day, our parents would be woken around 7a.m. by the sound of excitement from my younger sisters, having slept for only a few hours, and being 'surprised' at the presents they received from Santa.

Christmas dinner was special, with all ten of us there, and the turkey taking pride of place in the centre of the table. My father would lead in a prayer of thanksgiving and finish with 'Please God we will all be alive this time next year'. In the afternoon our parents would have a well-deserved nap in their chairs.

My father, Billy Burke, was an insurance agent with Irish Life and an agent for motor insurance. He travelled from village to village and house to house on his motorbike for over thirty years. He would sometimes renew car insurance for some clients who had not paid,

Home sweet home: Peter, Pat, Sheila, Ita and Liam with parents Eileen and Billy Burke.

Birthday boy: Liam Burke, celebrating his twenty-first with parents Eileen and Billy.

Helen Burke and Ann Behan.

New milking machines, Clongowes Wood College. Includes three Smyth brothers – Frank, Eugene, and Tom.

Eugene Smyth in the new milking parlour. Clongowes Wood College, 1949.

hoping that they would not let him down. However, he would not release the certificate until he was paid. One of these clients arrived at our doorstep on Christmas day, having been pulled over by the local garda on Christmas Eve, praying and hoping that my father had his car covered. However, when my father produced the certificate he immediately paid up and was most grateful, and it being the day it was, he was invited to have a glass of stout. My older sister, Helen, who was annoyed with this man calling on Christmas day, insisted on pouring out the bottle into the glass, and behind his back poured the contents of the salt cellar into the stout and handed it to him, wishing him a Happy Christmas. Being fond of the black stuff, he drank it down in one go, and having tasted the salt, jumped up and headed for the door. We were all bursting with laughter when we heard what happened, and Helen said, 'He won't forget to have his certificate next year'.

Clongowes Wood College gave a lot of employment to the people of Clane, Rathcoffey, Prosperous and Straffan, both in the college and on the farm, with over eighty men working there, and local girls were also employed. There were all sorts of workers, from tailors and bakers to farm labourers. The farm had over 800 acres of land, and Father Power was the manager. When we were in primary school, at the age of ten, we would go to the farm every Saturday from September to November and pick potatoes from 8a.m. to 6p.m. for 8s a day. There would be over forty lads working and it was hard-earned money. The length of drills was divided into twelve with pegs, and each team had three to four lads, depending on their age. The foreman was Michael Duffy from Richardstown and he would walk up and down the field roaring at us to hurry up. He in turn was under pressure from Father Power to dig out as many drills as possible for the least amount of money. Potatoes would be emptied from the basket into jute bags and the horse and cart would collect and bring them into the farmhouse. We would get a lunch break from one to two o'clock and had great fun playing in the hay barn or riding bicycles through the 'pleasure ground', where the priests walked reading their missals. One day, Seán McManmon was taking a corner at fifty miles an hour and rode straight into a priest, but before he got up off the ground, Seán was gone.

We also worked on the fruit farm picking raspberries and gooseberries, which was heaven compared to picking potatoes. Jimmy Nestor and his uncle, James Nestor, were in charge of the fruit with Iggie Cribbin, and we were paid according to the amount we picked.

We also thinned turnips and put the jute bags around our legs and tied them with twine at the ankles and over the knee. We would strike a rate with Father Power and I remember Gene Smyth telling us to go slow before agreeing a rate, to pretend to Father Power that the drills were tough. When the deal was done, we would fly through the drills. The farm workers were paid the minimum wage and worked very long hours. There was Jack McCabe looking after over one hundred pigs and bonhams, Tom Smyth was the farm manager, who planned the daily work with Father Power, while his brother, Frank, was in charge of the cows, bringing them in morning and evening for milking, and another brother, Eugene Smyth, also worked there. The Connolly brothers Peter, Jim and Paddy, as well as Francie and Jack Cribbin, Harry and Paddy Timmons, Tommy 'Tailor' Brilly, Jimmy Brilly, Jim Noonan, Tommy and Paddy McManmon, Kit Maloney and many others were employed in the college. Martin Connolly was the tailor, Nicholas Keary maintenance person and Michael Holligan chauffeured the clergy and students.

Clongowes Wood College.

The pleasure grounds, Clongowes Wood College.

As we got older, Paddy, Jim, Fergal Noonan and myself worked on the farm in Byrne's of Longtown during the summer for over five years and this was completely the opposite environment to Clongowes. Mr Andy Byrne, who owned the three-hundred-acre farm was a very generous man and treated all his employees with great respect. My first memory of Byrne's was when our neighbours Mrs Dodo Delaney and her son Seán worked there. Dodo worked in the house, and Seán on the farm. I remember Paddy and I working there in the

Roche's pub – Derry, Donadea.

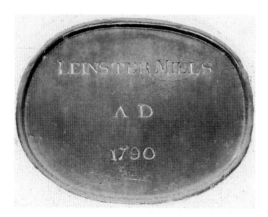

Plaque at Leinster Mills, Naas.

Nicholas Keary.

Turning the hay – Jack Connolly on Byrne's farm, Longtown.

Combine harvester in Byrne's farm.

late fifties, and Dodo bringing us out a bowl of soup, and I also remember being invited into the house to watch the Grand National on the BBC, which Nicholas Silver won. Mrs Molly Flanagan, Dodo's daughter, also worked there. I remember Peter Donnelly and Bill McGrath worked there too, and later Mr Byrne was privileged to have two great workmen, Paddy and Jack Connolly, who were employed there for many years, along with Willie Dunne. We did various types of work, from stacking bales of hay, and loading and unloading the trailers, to dividing the turnip seed plants for the combine, thinning turnips, and painting. There was great teamwork and Mr Byrne's son Anthony continued in the tradition of his father's goodwill after he passed away.

Many in the Clane area also worked in meat factories in Leixlip and Sallins, the mill in Celbridge, Odlum mills in Sallins and Leinster mills and Farringtons, Rathcoffey.

There were great characters in Clane: Paddy Stephens, Dinny Pegs, Dinny Fields, Jimmy Anderson, Cider Rourke, Joe Bibby, Phil Purcell, and Kathleen and Jimmy Dunne, among others.

Paddy Stephens lived in Ballinagappagh and was famous for snaring rabbits and selling them to locals and was fond of the odd bottle of stout. The sewerage came to Clane in 1957, and there was a six-foot-deep trench opened on the Doctor's road. Paddy was heading home late one night and fell into the trench – he waited for someone to come and shouted for help, and a good Samaritan helped him out and could find nothing wrong with him, but Paddy insisted that the ambulance be called, and was brought into Naas hospital and discharged later. Paddy took the County Council to court, but the judge fined Paddy for wasting his time and threw the claim out.

Dinny Fields was perhaps the best-known of these characters. He was always in good humour and loved meeting his mates for a pint in Jones', and his party piece was getting on his knees and barking like a dog. In the sixties there was dancing in Rathcoffey every Sunday, and when the National Anthem was coming to a close, Dinny would step up on the stage and conduct the band. He cycled from Rathcoffey to Clane daily and was always available to do small jobs in the village.

Paddy Casey was the turf man from Ballinafagh who travelled to Clane twice a week, hail, rain or snow with his horse and cart. He came to our house every Saturday to deliver two bags, and my mother always had a sandwich and a cup of tea for him. He would repay her with a few sods of turf, and he told us that in the late forties he would deliver turf to Dublin, leaving Ballinafagh at 4a.m., and returning at 9p.m. Paddy also liked his pint of Guinness and would call into Jones' after delivering all the turf and tying the horse to a pole. An hour or two later, he would climb into the cart and after a few words between the master and his horse he would lay back for a snooze and his horse would slowly take off and find his way safely home to Ballinafagh. Paddy later exchanged his horse for a donkey and he was sadly missed in the village when he ceased delivering.

Nurse Leddy was the district midwife who lived on the Dublin road opposite McKenna's shop and travelled all over the parish. She used to have a big bag and when we would see her coming we children would ask her had she any babies for us. She used tell us that there was a bus-load coming next week and we could all have one each. She was a very kind and generous lady and highly respected in the village.

Dr Michael Walsh, who lived on what we continue to call the Doctor's road (his house is now the Father John Sullivan Centre), was a great servant to the people of Clane and surrounding areas. He was available seven days a week and never complained when he was called out. He was a very private and religious person.

Sunday best. Jim Malone and his son. In the background, Pat Burke, Jimmy Dunne, Joe Bibby and Mick Giblin.

Dinny Fields: 'Legs Eleven'.

Clane GAA carnival fancy dress party, with Dinny Fields and Ned Coughlan. Robby Booth and Michael Giblin in the background.

Jack Kelly leaving Jones' pub with Miss Whelan in the background.

The barrel race of the pubs. Mick Walsh sat out this race. (In background).

Paddy Casey - Turfman at Butterstream, Clane

Clane, circa 1959.

The village in the fifties had three pubs: Manzor's, Jones', and Carroll's, and for a time there was also Maguire's. There were two drapery shops – Casey's and Goff's, two butchers – Bartle Smullen and Tom Byrne, and two bicycle shops – Peter Wallace and George Delaney. There were six or seven sweet and grocery shops. McKenna's, on the Dublin road, also sold hardware and gifts, as did Manzor's grocery, Lavin's (who with Blake's were also newsagents), Behan's, Jones' Grocery, Marron's, Dunn's and later residents Michael and Mary Daly. Jim Malone was the local barber.

Paddy Woods' Garage was perhaps the biggest in Kildare and an agent for Volkswagen, with over ten people employed there. Members of staff included Peter Sourke, Paddy Finan from Naas, Phil McCormack, Ned Coughlan, Danny Smyth, Timmy Coyne, Noel Kenny, Butsie Brereton, Jody Logan, Joe Leacy and Maureen Nolan in the office, and later Ger and Andy Gannon and Paddy Gibbons joined the staff.

The Post Office had Miss Theresa O'Neill as Postmistress and switchboard operator, who knew all the news from listening in on calls.

Other shops, offices and buildings included:

> Barton's Chemist
>
> Marron's Coalyard
>
> The Garda Station, which had a sergeant and three gardaí.
>
> Joe McCormack – Bookies
>
> Carey's Solicitor – beside Behan's Shop.
>
> Paddy Delaney – Capdoo, repaired shoes.

There was also a Courthouse in the village beside the old girls' school, which operated up to the late fifties.

'Any chance of a hot whiskey?' Dick Booth on his way home from work.

A man – and his bike inside. John Walsh, Butterstream.

Each household in the village had farm and yard workers as follows:

Manzor's – Larry Cribbin

Daly's – John Walsh. Lizzie Staunton worked in the house, and she also sold us cans of buttermilk and potatoes.

McEvoys – Pat Quinn

Convent - Jack Delaney and later Seán Cullen

Parish House - Tommy Campbell

Jones' – Paddy Archer

Dunn's – Billy Noble

Between 4 and 5p.m. every evening, the cows could be seen entering the village from all roads, at their leisure, walking to their milking parlours. They all disappeared from the roads by the mid-sixties, to give way to the Volkswagen, Morris Minor, Mini, Ford and the Massey Ferguson Tractor.

Manzor's also had a slaughterhouse, and we would see the animals being pushed and pulled in, before we would hear the sound of the gun. Then we would carry in the buckets of water to wash the blood off the floor while Bartle Smullen would get to work on the unfortunate animal. The butchers would carry the meat on their shoulders from the slaughterhouse to their premises in the village.

Blake's shop was one of the busiest in the village. It was a small two-storey thatched-roof house in the centre of the village where Londis is now, and Bridie Synnott worked there from 8a.m., when the newspapers arrived, until 9p.m. There was a small front door with a latch and you would have to bend your head when entering. The shop measured approximately

Back row: Garda James O'Donnell, Mai Fielding, and Garda Tom McGuinness. Front row: Paddy Lavin, George Delaney, James Geoghegan, Leo Butler. Photo taken outside Mai Fielding's shop (now Marie's Antiques) in 1949.

fifteen feet by twelve feet, but it was full of all kinds of sweets in big jars – bull's-eyes, toffees, jellies, chocolates, Liquorice Allsorts, Rum and Butter, and Scots Clan. You got twelve Nancy balls for 1d, and there were comics: *Beano, Dandy, Topper, Beezer,* and the girls bought *Bunty*.

There were two daily bread delivery vans from Boland's and Kelly's. Leo Butler from Naas worked for Boland's and Terry Byrne from Kilcock for Kelly's. Peter Shortt took over the Boland's van and Tom Darby for Kelly's. Tom also traded with St Brigid's Terrace residents, and every morning around 10.30a.m. the women would wait for Tom to drive up, park outside his residence and open the back door, releasing the beautiful smell of fresh bread and buns.

Our household bought all our groceries in Manzor's and every day from Monday to Saturday my mother would make out a list of what was required. Usually it was two pans, one pound of butter, half a pound of margarine, a quarter-pound of tea, two pounds of sugar, a pot of jam, a few Oxo and a packet of Rinso. Mr Manzor would write the items down and on Monday would hand me the bill to give to my mother, who would check it thoroughly, and after a day or two she would give me the money in an envelope to hand in. Mr Manzor would then give me a packet of biscuits for myself. He always arrived at our door on Christmas Eve with a present of a cake and a box of biscuits.

We purchased meat from Bartle Smullen, who also made his own black puddings. I remember the local dogs would wait outside the door for Bartle to throw out a bone.

Transport to and from Dublin was, for the vast majority, by bus. The first bus to Dublin was at 8.30a.m. and was known as 'the Edenderry bus' and the conductor was Wally. It was followed at 8.50a.m. by 'the Tullow Bus'. The 'paper bus' came in at 9.30a.m. and there would be customers waiting for it outside Lavin's and Blake's.

Off to a wedding – Lar and Rosie Cribbin, Capdoo.

Best pals: Martin Connolly, Lar Cribbin.

Kit Walsh, Lar Cribbin, Father Doyle, and a reek of turf in the background. Father Doyle's car reg. is IO – 6068.

Butcher – Bartle Smullen.

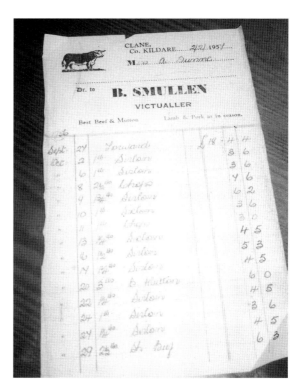

Bill Heading.

MEMORIES OF COUNTY FINALS

There was only one true sport in every household in Clane and that was Gaelic football. Clane GAA Club was and continues to be one of the best in the county. In the fifties, when the team's 'changing rooms' – as was the case in ninety-nine per cent of all pitches in Ireland – was the corner of Manzor's field, the determination and will to win were as strong as they are today. The seven-a-side annual tournament at Rathcoffey was one we all looked forward to, and the fitness of the teams was unbelievable in those times.

There were excellent teams from Kilcock, with Paddy and Fred Gibbons, Davey Dalton, Larry McCormack, Bobby O'Connell and Tommy Hanrahan in goals. There was a fantastic UCD team that included the great Kevin Beahan and Gabriel Kelly; there was the Air Corps from Baldonnell, and the mighty Rhode, Edenderry, Raheens, Carbury and Maynooth teams. But Clane – with Pa and Seamie Connolly, Dessie in goals, Danny and Frank Smyth, Jim O'Donnell and Tommy Merriman – were our heroes, and there would be huge excitement on the sideline, with the spectators half-way out on the pitch roaring their teams on and the unfortunate linesman trying to keep them back on the line.

Kildare won the Leinster Final in 1956, beating Wexford, with Des Marron in the Kildare goals. I remember that Sunday evening and seeing Paddy Gibbons and Des in the village. There was no huge celebration like today, as most of those lads had to report for work on the following day.

Des and his wife Kathleen were married in September 1959, and I had the privilege of serving the Mass, which was at 10a.m. Clane were playing Round Towers two weeks later in the county final – Clane's first appearance in the final for over forty years. So as the team assembled in the hall on the Saturday night before the final, the hall door opened and Des arrived back from his honeymoon, to support the team. Unfortunately for Des, the Towers team won the final, scoring five goals…

However, one of the greatest memories I have is of the 1963 final: the great Seán Conneff trained the team, and under the stewardship of Clane's greatest mentors – Seán Cribbin, Joe Bracken and Bill Merriman – and with Pa as captain, they got their revenge on Round Towers, winning 1-8 to 2-1. What sportsmanship, to see members of the Round Towers team carry Pa on their shoulders. The bonfires were burning on the green, and celebrations went on for over a week; many pioneers had to take their pins down that week.

The 1967 final against Carbury was unbelievable. Carbury were going for their third championship in a row and were favourites, but Clane now had the great Tommy Carew, and of course Pa, and most of the '63 line-up, with young Phil McCormack coming in to replace Des who had retired. Carbury took control from the start and looked like all-over winners, and with ten minutes to go were leading 1-9 to 1-5. Clane were playing with fourteen men, as J.J. Langan had been sent off. The wise Seán Cribbin and Joe Bracken went to work: Tommy Carew came out to midfield and was fouled, Pa took the free, and Andy Hughes finished to the net. One point down, Tommy Carew levels the score, Paddy Bracken takes a sideline, and again Hughes catches the ball, turns, and drives to the net. Clane in front, Pa kicks a fifty straight to the net and Clane wins by six points. Carbury were on their knees, not knowing what hit them – another great celebration in the village of Clane.

Clane team, the 1963 champions.

Clane GAA on tour, London 1963. Back row: Jim O'Donnell, Martin McCormack, Dick Flanagan, Joe Bracken, Peter Marron. Front row: Seán Conneff, Seán Cribbin, George Harrington, Paddy Harrington, Seamie Connolly, Tommy Connolly – and is that Pa with an accordion?

Clane GAA, London 1963. Jimmy Casey, Martin Connolly, Pa Connolly, Seán Conneff, Paddy Harrington, J.J. Langan.

The Great Comeback: the 1963 final. Andy Hughes celebrates with Jim O'Donnell after scoring a goal in the closing minutes, while Carbury goalie Ollie Crinnigan looks on in amazement.

I have been following Kildare all my life and remember many frustrating occasions in the sixties, travelling to Croke Park and seeing great Kildare teams just being edged out by Offaly and Meath teams who went on to win All-Irelands – but one delightful memory was in the Leinster Championship, when Kildare were playing Meath. Meath had the 'tough' Red Collier, who played in the backs, and the ball was heading towards the side-line near the Cusack stand. Red was running from his back line and Pa was going forward, both saw each other approaching and they collided, shoulder to shoulder, and the crowd of over 60,000 came to their feet when the great Red went, like a bag of spuds, crashing to the ground.

CLANE CYCLING CLUB – UNITED ROAD CLUB

It is hard to believe how popular cycling was in Ireland in the late fifties and early sixties, and Clane was no exception. There would be hundreds of people lining the street to see our local heroes. The big names were Dublin's Shay O'Hanlon, Seamus Kennedy, Ben McKenna (Meath), Gene Mangan (Kerry), and for me the best of them all was Kildare's Paddy Flanagan. Clane had a very strong club with Murt Logan, Jim and Seán Halligan, Seán Delaney, Fergal Lee, Tommy and Paddy McManmon, and Paddy and Christy Connolly.

Later the United Road Club was formed, which included Vincent Burke, Liam Baxter, (Kilcullen), Mick Donoghue (Carlow) and Vincent Sheridan (Kilcock). The man who worked hard behind the scene was Patsy Farrell, the chairman, who was also very much involved with the Kildare team in the famous Rás Tailteánn. Dick Flanagan, Mick McAndrew (Rathcoffey), and George Delaney were also very much involved, and Mick organised races for beginners in Rathcoffey.

There were many big races in Clane, with over one hundred top-class riders from all over the country participating. The race would start outside Carroll's pub on the Prosperous road, continue up to Firmount, turn left for Millicent, and out to Bodenstown Cross, turning left back into Clane. There would be up to twelve laps, with the finish outside the old girls' school on the Main Street. A huge crowd would assemble on the corner and there was great excitement to see a Clane man leading the field.

Murt Logan was a first-rate cyclist and was on the Kildare team for over eight years. He was chosen on the Irish five-man team to compete in France in 1963. Shay O'Hanlon was regarded as number one in Ireland but on more than one occasion, Murt beat him. The *Evening Press* sport pages had the following heading: 'Thrilling win for Logan', and it reported:

'In a thrilling sprint finish by ten riders, all Ireland 100 miles champion, Murt Logan of Clane CC won the Memorial Cycle race in the Phoenix Park. The twenty-one year-old had only inches to spare over Seamus O'Hanlon. Logan literally lifted his machine with some power pedalling over the line for one of the finest and hardest fought wins seen in the Park for many a day. Logan, who rode for Kildare in this year's Rás Tailteánn and also won the Tour of the Mournes, was immediately congratulated by O'Hanlon.'

Dick Flanagan shows his delight as Murt Logan crosses the finishing line at a race in Clane.

The Ras Tailteánn 1963, going through Clane.

Above: Cill Dara Ras Tailteánn team, 1962: Murt Logan, Jim Halligan, Eamon Ryan, Liam Baxter, Hal Conway, Ned Flanagan, Patsy Farrell, and Vince Burke.

Right: Charles J. Haughey, then a minister, presenting the Seán Lemass trophy to Murt Logan.

Murt won many big races, including Rás Gaillimhe and the thirty-two kilometre Meath Race, in which he beat Paddy Flanagan, but one of his proudest moments was when he was presented by Charlie Haughey – then a minister – with the Seán Lemass Trophy in the one-hundred mile race in the Phoenix Park in 1962.

Jim Halligan cycled with the Clane Club for over ten years and was a great team member who did all the hard work for his team-mates and represented the Kildare team in the Rás Tailteánn. He tells the story that at one big race, himself and one of the country's best cyclists, Seamus Kennedy, broke away from the main bunch. Usually a duo would work together to keep in front, but Jim realised that Kennedy was not doing his bit and staying on Jim's wheel. After another ten miles Jim had had enough, so he took the pump off his bike, and as Kennedy decided to break from Jim, he was landed in the ditch.

Clane United Road Club was very successful and won the All Ireland gold medal four-man team award in 1963 with Murt Logan, Jim Halligan, Vincent Burke and Liam Baxter. Cycle racing must go down as one of the toughest sports. My brother, Vince, started the sport when he was eighteen years old, and every spare penny he had went into parts for the bike. He would arrive home from work on a summer's evening, put on his gear and head off for the Sallygap, returning three hours later, his clothes wet with sweat, and then he would have his dinner. He would cycle up to five evenings a week, and on Sunday take part in a cycle race, which might have been held in any part of the country, and the distance of the race could be one hundred kilometres. He drank a pint of Jersey milk every day, the bottle with the green top, with plenty of cream on top. He now lives in Perth, Australia, and continues to cycle up to sixty miles a week.

CLANE TABLE TENNIS CLUB

Clane Table Tennis Club was founded in 1958 in the hall and its founder members were Peter Duffy, Leo Carroll, Johnny and Hugh O'Connor (Rathcoffey), Chrissie Brilly and Patty Doyle.

There was a club in Rathcoffey that ceased playing, and the tables were purchased from them. Gene Smyth, Michael Bracken, Vincent Burke, Leo Carroll, Philip and Kevin O'Neill, Mick and Louis Connolly, Larry Higgins, Moira Burke, Breeda Behan, Breda and Claire O'Donnell, Marjorie Bracken and Vera Higgins were also very prominent early members.

Table Tennis became a craze, and clubs were formed all over the county: in Prosperous, Coill Dubh, Naas, Kill, Newbridge, Maynooth, Kildare, and Kilcullen, and other very popular clubs included Enfield and Abbeyleix.

There were four divisions of eight teams in the mid sixties, and Clane were represented in each division. Clane produced some great players, both male and female, and without doubt the best was Frankie Behan, a left-handed player who won many individual trophies in the top section and won many more with Robbie Booth, his doubles partner, and Kathleen Mahony in the mixed doubles. Behind all good clubs are great people, and one of these was Peter Duffy, who did tremendous work for the club, which had over eighty members at its peak. There was great friendship between clubs, and after a match refreshments would be provided, and depending on the club visiting, it might end up with a bit of a sing-song. Teams from Kill and Kildare had such functions, and Peter McManmon would be the life and soul, singing Jim Reeves' famous song 'He'll Have to Go'.

Table tennis club, 1972: Back row: Jim Mahony, Peadar and Pauric McCormack. Middle row: Paddy McManmon, Robby Booth, Peter Duffy, Frankie Behan, Liam Burke. Front row: Breeda McIntyre, Rita McCormack, Margaret Donagher, Peggy Higgins, Margaret Cullen, and Ann Smyth.

The wedding of Frank Behan and Mai Shortt (1974). Guard of honour, clockwise: Peter Duffy, Paddy Behan, Liam Burke, and Bobbie Booth.

1967 Kildare Table Tennis Awards, familiar faces from Clane and Prosperous. Back row: Charlie Dunny, Seán McCormack, Shay Curry, Stan McManmon. Third row: Simon Behan, Liam Burke, Robbie Booth, Frank Behan, Peadar McCormack. Second row: Peter Duffy, Marjorie Bracken, Mary Healy, Mary Ward. Front row: Pamela Duffy, Margaret Duffy, Kathleen Mahony.

The annual Christmas party was held in the hall for over six years and it was always packed, never any trouble like today, just complete enjoyment. The hall would be decorated with holly, balloons and bunting. Refreshments were provided in the back kitchen with Mrs Jo Mahony, Mrs Lil McCormack and Mrs Nan McCormack helping out. The kitchen had a huge open fire, with large kettles on the hob constantly boiling. Eileen Tiernan looked after the ladies' cloakroom, while Jimmy Dunne kept a watchful eye in the gents'.

I remember one of those parties; the Calandos Showband was playing, there was a huge storm, and trees were blown down all around the area. The band arrived at around 8p.m. to set themselves up, when all of a sudden the lights went out and we were all left in the dark. We darted out to see was there any light from McEvoy's house, but it was also out. Gene Smyth and Peter Duffy got into the car, went down to Blake's shop and Bridie produced all the big red candles that were left over from the Christmas. Then on to Lavin's and Jones' grocery shops for more candles, and inside an hour the hall and stage were lit up with candles, as were the toilets and kitchen. The whole scene was so seasonal and romantic, and the Calandos played a stormer in front of over 250 party-goers, with John Egan on the drums, Percy Jones on the trumpet and Mick Lawlor singing as loud as possible, the night proved to be the best and most enjoyable ever held.

Bryan Sammon and Liam Burke in *Toff and the Tramp*, 1969.

CLANE YOUTH CLUB DRAMA

We staged a number of comedies, but the best was *Troubled Bachelors*, a play in three acts, in 1966. The three bachelors were Bryan Sammon, Jim Byrne and myself, and the play also included Liz Higgins, Pauline Murray, Camilla O'Neill, Mai Shortt, Pat Harty, Jim Mahony, Phil McCormack and Simon Behan – who played the part of a messenger boy. There was also a supporting programme that included members of Staplestown Youth Club, Lily Tuite, Ann Casey and Cáit Murphy, who were accompanied by Father Tom O'Malley on guitar.

Another play in which Jim Byrne and myself acted, and which Joe Noonan directed, was about a goat, and at the rehearsal we had lads imitating a goat in the background. Joe, being the perfect director, asked around Clane about acquiring a goat, with little success. But on the day of the play, Jim Byrne arrived from the Doctor's road with a goat in tow and with a little persuasion brought it into the hall and left it in the gent's toilet. When the time came to go on stage we lifted it on and everything was going smoothly until the goat decided that he also wanted to perform – and the audience went hilarious, when right in the centre of the stage he went to the toilet. A supporting group who were called Purple Dust included Pat Burke, Frankie and Simon Behan and Stan McManmon. They were dressed hippy-style and mimed to a record, which was placed behind the stage. The song played was 'Glad All Over' and everything was going well until Stan decided to jump up and down to the fast beat, and with the vibrations, the needle also jumped, leaving the famous Purple Dust stranded on stage. Another record came on and when Simon Behan started swinging the microphone in his hand around like a lasso, the head came off and flew into the audience, missing Mrs Ahern, who was sitting in the front row, by inches.

We hired the sound equipment from Noel Mongey, Naas. Three microphones and speakers, and they were all connected to one socket. On one occasion we were over-enthusiastic and borrowed more speakers but with the hall filled to capacity, the fuse went and the place was in darkness. Matches were struck all over the hall and one torch was found. Panic started to set in, but Simon Behan, our electrician and back-stage manager, came to the rescue and the show went on.

Staplestown Youth Club held their weekly hop every Wednesday and we in Clane had a very friendly and close relationship with them.

There remains a great bond, which now goes back forty years, with members of both Youth Clubs. Clane Youth and Table Tennis Clubs amalgamated, and St Brigid's club was formed. We continued to have the hops up to 1969, and it was at one of these that I had a date with my future wife Patti, whom I first met when she worked in Odlums Laboratory during the harvest of 1968. Being the 'slow and shy' type, it took me a long time to ask her out. The table tennis continued up to the late seventies and played a huge part for the youth of Clane.

CLANE LAWN TENNIS CLUB

Bryan's father, Tommy Sammon, had a large lawn, which is now the entrance road to Liffey Lawns, and in the mid-sixties he erected a tennis court – using chicken mesh wire as the net, but it was marked out to perfection and mowed and rolled as often as required. We played tennis all summer and included Breda and Denise Langan, (who both later became Lady Captains of Naas LTC), Gertie, Jacinta and Fidelma Connolly, and Miriam Ferris. There were also the usual Clane lads: Paddy, Bryan, Jim Mahony, Peter O'Neill and myself.

Tennis was also played in Charlie O'Neill's, Abbeylands. In 1972 Des Marron was approached by Clongowes Wood College and asked if anyone was interested in using their tennis courts during the summer. Des contacted Bryan and a meeting was arranged for a delegation to meet in Clongowes the following Sunday after Mass. Des, Bryan, Peter O'Neill, Liz Higgins and myself met with Father Percy Winders, and an agreement was made that we form Clane Lawn Tennis Club, and courts would be available during the college holidays and at certain times daily for the remainder of the year. A meeting was held in Clane GAA Club in June 1972, and

Clane's own Morris Minor.

Clane Lawn Tennis Club, the winners. Back row: Andrew Curran, Enda Behan, Trevor Beale, Tommy McAndrew, Owen Fennell. Front row: Ronan Behan, Ritchie Mahony, Christine O'Reilly, Karen O'Reilly, Aoife Malone, Sheila Lynch, Noreen Priestly, and Margaret Mahony.

Lawn tennis, before the club was formed, 1964. Left to right: Liam Burke, Paddy Behan, Breda Langan, Bryan Sammon.

Clane Lawn Tennis Club was formed and we never looked back. Committee members also included Paddy and Peter Duffy. The first match was played against a Celbridge team and the Clane team were: Ladies – Sorcha and Roma Nevin (Prosperous), Mary Kelly and Liz Higgins. Men – Bryan, Padraig Daly (Prosperous), Peter O'Neill and myself. Then Mick Hennessy, Gerry Walsh, Dave Mahon and John Kelly became involved and in a few weeks almost one hundred members joined, and the Tuesday night tournament commenced and continues to this day. Mick and Paddy organised a club league with four men's and three ladies' divisions, with twelve in each division. This was run over the summer months for three years and was a huge success. The club had twelve great years in Clongowes, and when the Parish land became available in the old boys' school, the club purchased it for £6,500, which was raised by offering sixty-five life memberships for £100 each, which was a lot of money at that time. The new Club ground was opened in 1985 and is now one of the best in the country, and in fact won the 'All-Ireland Club of the Year' in 2004.

III

HORSE RACING, EMIGRATION AND LOCAL POLITICS

Liam Burke

When we were young, racing around the fields, we called ourselves after local horses and others that were famous: Shower of Silver (which was owned by Peter Coonan, from Mainham), Clane Beau, and Ned Cash's horses – You Mind Me and Chimney Smoke. Other horses included Mr What and Quare Times. In 1958 and 1959, at a point-to-point in Two Mile House Chimney Smoke won two races on the same day: the first and last race, with Jim Cash riding on both occasions. On 14 March 1959 the *Leinster Leader* also reported that Ned Jnr rode the third horse, Quel Damage and Charlie O'Neill rode the fourth, Sullivan III.

Peter McCreery came to Clane at that time and Joe Bracken Jnr left school to join him, followed shortly after by Christo McCormack. Year after year many followed in their footsteps, including Peadar McCormack, Mick Ryan, Tony and Pascal (Ginner) McManmon. Larry Higgins was also very much involved, and he owned a horse there called Moneen, which won some good races. Peter had great horses, like Mr Moonlight, Santo Domingo, Mount Parson, Bonne, Dromore and Seskin Bridge. Joe Bracken rode Tarquin Bid in the Aintree Grand National and was well up with the leaders until they came down at Beechers on the second round. The best horse was Hilly Way, which Ted Walsh rode, and it won big races in Cheltenham and Aintree. Ted also rode other great horses from the McCreery stables – Castleruderry and Daring Run. Peter Jnr, who rode many winners, continued in his father's footsteps and went on to win the Irish Grand National with the grey Son of War.

EMIGRATION

In the mid-sixties a few young men from Clane realised that there was money to be made on the other side of the Atlantic. George and Denis Ross, Philip O'Neill, Kevin O'Neill and Louis Connolly, who were very much involved with the Clane community, decided to make the break and were later joined by Gene and Toby Smyth, (Mainham) and Gerry O'Neill (brother of Charlie). These young men have to be applauded for having the courage to take such a gamble and it must have been a huge ordeal for their families. They sailed from Ireland to Toronto, which took over five weeks.

The only one to come back was George Ross, who met his wife Joan Bradley, from Naas, in Vancouver. George invested his earnings in farm supplies, and Ross Grain and did a thriving business. The other lads, who are now all in their early sixties, are settled with their extended

At the Galway races, 1973. Proprietors of Lydon House, Galway, making a presentation to Peter McCreery (trainer of Moneen, winner of Lydon House hurdle). Bobby Coonan (jockey), Lord Killanin (on the right), Larry Higgins (owner, back right).

families, and I'm sure they can't believe how the village has changed since their departure. Another great friend, Michael Ross, also joined his brothers in the US but returned to Ireland to join the priesthood, and now resides with the Salesian Order in Maynooth. Billy Smyth emigrated to Germany and joined the US Air Force, and he now resides in the USA. Other great community members who left for foreign pastures when they were in their twenties were Peter McManmon, who resides in England, and our great school friends Seán Farrell, who was the Loughanure football captain, and John Langan, also in England and the Richardstown Football captain. Billy Barrett took the long road to Australia. My brother Vince emigrated to Perth, Australia, where he now resides with his family. My sister, Sheila Lynam, is living it up in Brussels, and like so many others who left this country, my brother and sister are now in a position to return for holidays.

The above were those whom we knew closely, so one can imagine the many hundreds and thousands who left the Clane area and our beloved country in the fifties and sixties to seek work – and here we are now with a complete turn-around, with over 200,000 coming from all over the world to work in Ireland in the past three years.

Teresa Brayton wrote that great Kildare song 'The Old Bog Road' – which is situated on the Kilcock-Enfield road – and I'm sure many Clane emigrants are familiar with the following:

Moneen (no.4), ridden by Bobby Coonan, clears the last hurdle to win at Galway.

Joe Bracken on Tarquin Bid no.25 at Beechers Brook in the Aintree Grand National 1973. Red Rum, no. 7, went on to win the race.

My feet are here in Broadway, this blessed harvest morn,
But oh the ache that's in them for the spot where I was born.
Had I the chance to wander back or own a king's abode,
'Tis soon I'd see the hawthorn tree down the old bog road.

THE BEAUTIFUL VILLAGE OF CLANE

I've travelled the high-ways
and been down the by-ways
while walking through sunshine and rain
but my memories ne'er lack
as my thoughts go back
on the beautiful village of Clane.

Chorus

To Clane, Clane, I'll go again
to stroll by the river
that I should have left never.
And there I'll repose
when the evening will close
on the beautiful village of Clane.

Those years of great joy
when I roamed as a boy
on the banks of the Liffey spent playing.
Oh, the nights of the dance
and of youth's young romance
in the beautiful village of Clane.

Chorus

From youth, I grew older
my heart, it grew bolder
and longed to be over the mane.
And on life's weary road
I have carried my load
far, far, from the village of Clane.

Chorus

Tomorrow I'm leaving
this land where I'm grieving
returning to Dara's green plain.

In my heart is the joy
which I knew as a boy
in the beautiful village of Clane.

Arranged by Maureen McCormack, words by Kevin Lynch

POLITICS

My earliest memory of politics is having a day off school when an election took place, as the school was the polling station.

Clane was like most other areas in Ireland where everyone knew who voted for who, and families who voted for Fianna Fáil would not be friendly with those who were Fine Gael and vice versa, but thankfully, those days have long since passed – or have they?

I remember the coalition government of the late fifties, when Kildare had two ministers: Gerry Sweetman (Fine Gael) and Billy Norton (Labour). When an election was coming up, we used to hear the following:

Did you see or did you pass
Billy Norton on an ass.
Gerry Sweetman on his tail,
Shouting up for Fine Gael

In the mid-sixties, Patrick Norton took over the seat that his father had held for years, but before the following general election he decided to leave the Labour party and go independent. He then applied to join Fianna Fáil, and the Clane cumann debated in Dillon's Pub whether they would vote for him to be accepted. Paddy Behan and I were outside, sitting on the windowsill, and there was uproar inside. Dinny Colgan, who was a staunch Fianna Fáil member, shouted that they should not allow a traitor into the party, and it became a free-for-all, with everyone shouting each other down. It was like listening to Frank Hall's *Ballymagash*. Dick Flanagan, who

Dinny Colgan, Firmount.

chaired the meeting, could be heard shouting 'order, order', and eventually a motion was passed that Norton be accepted as a candidate in the next election. He lost his seat.

Kildare County Council elections were held in the mid-sixties, and Fine Gael nominated Oliver Reilly (Prosperous) to stand for the party. He travelled all over North Kildare, canvassing from door to door. At 7p.m. on election day he noticed from the voting sheet that a Fine Gael voter, Marjorie Malone of Digby Bridge, had not cast her vote. He was informed that she was a student in Dublin and could not come down to vote, so he organised for his son Seán to travel up to Dublin to collect her, and two minutes before the polling station closed she arrived in Prosperous to vote. Oliver won the seat by one vote and remained a councillor for many years, and Seán occupied the same seat for a further twenty years.

Candidates would address those coming out of church on Sunday, and Charlie O'Neill Snr would provide a tractor and trailer for the Fine Gael man, while Kit Walsh would provide a lorry for Fianna Fáil. No one could hear what they were saying, but the faithful followers would hang around the church rails until they had finished talking and give them a bit of applause.

Bodenstown Sunday was always a big occasion before the Northern Ireland troubles, and as children we used to walk there to enjoy the bands and marchers, and in Sallins the stalls were lined up along the road selling chocolates, fruit, and sandwiches and it was a lovely family day out.

In 1972, Paddy and I and a few others drove up to Dublin to march in protest against Bloody Sunday, from Parnell Square to the British Embassy in Merrion Square. The march was organised by the trade unions, and over 50,000 turned out. As we were walking over O'Connell Bridge, we realised that Sinn Féin members had hijacked the event and were shouting 'Jack Lynch out', and so on. When the embassy was set on fire with petrol bombs the gardaí were powerless, and we decided to get out as quickly as possible. As we jumped over the steel rails in Merrion Square, a spike went up through Paddy's shoe. Running back, we realised he was in pain but we managed to get back to the car and headed for home. On the way, we paid a visit to the doctor to bandage the wounded foot and then to the cobbler, Paddy Delaney (Capdoo), for a new sole on the shoe.

> Like as the waves make towards the pebbled shore,
> So do our minutes hasten towards their end.
> Each changing place with that which goes before,
> In sequent toil all forwards do contend.

You're Welcome Patsy

Patsy Larkin, butcher, came to Clane in 1959 to work for John Lawless, who had taken over from Bartle Smullen at Manzor's Corner. He lodged in Manzor's house under the tender care of Mrs Manzor, and on his first evening he entered the bar, a complete stranger. He sat himself up for a drink and in those days when a stranger entered a public premises, the locals would eye them up. Tommy Mahony approached Paddy and introduced himself and when Patsy told Tommy who and what he was, Tommy said 'you're welcome to Clane, Patsy' and enquired if he had ever played darts, as they were playing another team and were short a man. Paddy explained that he would love to play but had never thrown a dart before. 'Well,' says Tommy, 'no time like the present, come over here and I will introduce you to the lads on the team'. They were Seamie Connnolly, Paddy Bracken, and Paddy and Tommy McManmon.

Pleased to 'meat' you Ma'am. Patsy Larkin and Lil McCormack.

Three FCA men, Tommy McManmon on the left and Tommy Casey on the right

Dodo and Seán Delaney, Mr Kelly, and Jimmy Dunne (in the background) going to Mass.

After a few more sessions with these lads, friendships grew and Patsy decided there and then that Clane was the place to be. He set up his own business in 1961, and when Tom Byrne — who had a butcher's shop in the centre of the town — retired in 1967, Patsy took over, built a new shop and house there in 1970 and ran a great business for a further twenty-five years.

THE VILLAGE IN 1956

Lavin's Grocery/Newsagent

Peter Wallace Bicycles/Batteries

Garda Station

Geoghegans

Doyle's House/Farmyard

George Delaney Bicycle Repairs

Byrne — Butcher

O'Neill's — Ulster Bank

Jones' — Bar/Grocery/Farmyard

Post Office — Dunns

Maguire's Bar

Joe McCormack — Bookies

Goff's Drapery

Dalton's

Barton's Chemist

Marron's Petrol Station/Shop

Carroll's Bar/Farmyard

Ladies Hairdresser

McKenna's — Shop, Dublin Road

Parish Hall

Dunn's (Miss Gibbon's Sweet shop)

Woods' Garage/Petrol Station

Manzor's Bar/Grocery/Farmyard

Bartle Smullen Butcher

Daly's House/Farmyard

Blake's Shop — Sweets/Newsagent

Casey's — Ladies' Drapery

McEvoy's — House/Farmyard

Parish Church

Convent/ Farmyard

Girls' National School

Court House

Marron's House/Farmyard/Coal

Fr Doyle PP House

Behan's Shop/House

Carey — Solicitor

Frost's House

Cash's House/Stablesv

Boys' School

King's Meeting Room.

ESTATES

Stream — 6 houses

St Brigid's Terrace — 12 houses.

SAINT MICHAEL AND ALL ANGELS CHURCH, MILLICENT

The church stands on a rising ground in a prominent and central position in the parish, and its tower is visible for a considerable distance on all sides. The dressings of the windows and doors, the arches, and the pillars are of white Bath stone. The steps, pulpit base, and platform are of Portland stone, and the external steps and bowl of font are of granite. The walls throughout are lined with brick. The roof is of pitch-pine covered with Welsh slates, and the doors, floor, and fittings are of Riga oak. The external walls are of ashlar, giving the idea of great strength and solidity. The principal rafters, solid and richly carved, are of a semicircular shape. They have intersecting purlins and deeply carved bosses at the intersections, which make a wagon-form framework. Above the baptistery in the west wall is a wheel window, filled with richly coloured glass. The church was consecrated by Archbishop Trench in 1883.

On 22 March 1947 Nurse Mary Stack, on night duty at St Conleth's Sanatorium, saw a glare in the sky in the direction of St Michael's Church and called the Clane gardaí, who on arrival at the church found the centre section on fire. The Curragh fire brigade saved the nave and part of the chancel. The vestry, choir stalls, organ and tower were destroyed.

The work of reconstruction started in 1949, and was completed in 1951, costing £36,000. We in Clane remember with great fondness Archdeacon Brian Handy and his wife, who were very much involved with the Clane ICA. Rev. Handy was instituted rector of the Parish in 1934, and in 1960 became Archdeacon of Kildare. He retired in 1974 and died on 14 July 1976. He was also father of the now famous writer, lecturer and broadcaster Charles Handy.

St Michael and All Angels, Millicent, the interior of the church.

Above and below: Church of St Michael and All Angels, Millicent.

Above: Martha Behan's shop.

Below: Hewetson School.

Main street, Clane.

IV

PA CONNOLLY

Seamus Mahony

Pa Connolly played all his football for Clane. He won medals at all grades and Under-14 and Under-18. He was captain of the Minors in 1954 when they won the League, and in 1955, when they won the County Championship. He went on to play Senior Football for Clane at the age of seventeen and played his first Senior game with the county at the age of nineteen, against Meath in Conleth's Park, Newbridge, playing at mid-field.

Pa played some great games for Kildare in the late fifties and sixties and was then chosen to play for the Railway Cup Leinster Team in 1962, 1963, 1964 and 1965. He played left fullback in all those games.

He was also picked as an All Star Award winner on 16 March 1964. The presentation was held in the Gresham Hotel, Dublin. In 1965 Pa was selected along with twelve other players from the thirty-two counties to travel to New York and play in the Cardinal Cushing Games.

Pa was voted the player of the tournament and was presented with a gold watch by Senator Bobby Kennedy. He was recognised as one of the best backs ever to play for Kildare or Leinster, but he loved to play football for his local club team. He captained Clane when they won their first championship in forty-five years in 1963, and he then captained them to win in 1967 and 1975. Everyone thought Pa was finished playing then, but in 1977 he was captain when they won the Leinster Leader Cup, beating Raheens in the final. Pa was carried off the pitch by the Raheens' players after the match and won the Man of the Match Award. He was voted Senior Club Footballer of the Year in 1975.

PA'S HEROES

In the year '67 on September 17
We travelled to Newbridge all eager and keen
To see Champions Carbury and Challengers Clane
Do battle to find where the title would reign.

Allenwood, Raheens and Moorefield were hailed
But before Mangan's men all their best efforts failed
The Scribes and the Judges in general felt
That Carbury would add the Clane scalp to their belt.

The two greats: Pa Connolly receives the Senior Championship Cup from Bill Merriman, September 1963.

Tom and Jim Mahony.

The first minutes of play saw some Carbury attacks
Which were all driven off by our vigilant backs
A point by O'Donnell first blood for the day
And some minutes later a goal by J.J.

A point from Carew we were playing with great will
Five points to our credit to Carbury's nil
But Mangan's men now were all finding their feet
Their fielding and speed wasn't easy to beat.

The Carbury fight back wasn't to be ignored
As point after point they put up on the board
When the first half had ended 'twas they had the spares
For our boys' left the field with two points in arrears.

The second half saw them forge further ahead
And the loyal Clane supporters were greatly in dread
That their team would at long last be forced for to yield
  Like Allenwood, Raheens and the lads from Moorefield.

Four points in arrears with ten minutes to go
We feared that we'd ne'er see our bonfires aglow
But the mighty 'Pa' Connolly now reigning supreme
  Called for a last desperate stand from his team.

'Twas the spirit of famous Clane men of the past
Who had pinned our flag high at the top of the mast
The message inspiring was simple and plain
Do or die but bring honour and glory to Clane.

And now 'twas the Carbury men's turn to fret
As the bould Andy Hughes slammed the ball in the net
And a few moments later Carew levelled up
With a beautiful shot – a point nearer the Cup.

We had the Carbury men groggy as they fumbled and groped
For the long final whistle they earnestly hoped
Like a boxer who welcomes the tone of the bell
For our lads playing like devils were giving them hell.

We swarmed all over the brave Carbury men
And Hughes on the mark had a major again
A goal in the lead with time ticking away
We were confident now that we'd carry the day.

Pa's heroes: the Clane team of '67. Back row: W. Burcheal W. Cooney, E. Heffernan, M. Cooney, Tony Carew, L. Higgins, N. Delaney, J.J. Langan, T. Connolly, P. Bracken, T. Mahony. Front row: J. Higgins, P. Lynch, A. Hughes, P. McCormack, Tommy Carew, P. Connolly, R. Kinahan, D. Smyth, S. Connolly, J. Mahony.

A Carbury kick out 'twas a fair longish punt
As they desperately tried for to keep in the hunt
But their midfield man fouled, and the ball it was set
And the 'Pa' sent direct to the back of the net.

The day it is ours – Oh! Listen to that roar
Reminiscent of famous Clane victories of yore
When Merriman, Cribbin, Bracken and Losty
Played football that was a delight for to see.

The game it is over it's now history
And the name of 'Pa' Connolly a legend will be
His feats on the field will forever remain
An example to all and a credit to Clane.

Oh here's to our lads, they're the cause of our joy
Who by their great victory have our flags waving high
Loudly we hail them, and proudly we raise
Our glasses to toast them on their day of days.

Pat Behan
(1919-1973)

V

MEMORIES OF FATHER JOHN SULLIVAN (1861-1933)

Conor Harper, SJ

The name of the Servant of God, Father John Sullivan SJ has been familiar to the people of Clane for the past one hundred years. For most of his priestly life, Father John lived at Clongowes Wood College. He joined the Jesuit community shortly after his ordination to the priesthood on 28 July 1907. From the beginning the people of Clane recognised that a special priest was among them.

The journey of life is full of surprises – and the experience of John Sullivan is no exception. He was born in Eccles Street, Dublin on 8 May 1861, and allowing for his family background, the beginnings of his life foreboded future comfort and respectability. His father, Edward, was already a successful barrister, showing the signs of what was to be a brilliant future success in life. His mother, Elizabeth Bailey, came from a prominent family in Passage West in County Cork. The Sullivans came from Mallow. The Baileys were Catholics, and the Sullivans Protestants.

The history of the Sullivan family of Mallow is interesting. It would seem that John's great-grandfather, James, had very close connections with the Jephson Norreys family of Mallow Castle. He had been baptised a Catholic but on his marriage to a Protestant, Mary Fitzgerald, in 1782, it is evident that he either decided to convert to the Established Church or at least that he consented to allow his children to be brought up as Protestants. However, on his deathbed he was reconciled to the Catholic Church by the local parish priest, Father Thomas Barry.

State and church papers give an astonishing account of the funeral of James Sullivan on 19 January 1814 (a few short months before the opening of Clongowes as a school). The state Papers (the originals of which were tragically destroyed in the Custom House fire in 1922) note 'Funeral, complaints of priests [sic] conduct at, corpse carried away by a mob at Mallow, Mass said and harangue delivered at Churchyard' (State Papers, Series I 1790-1831). The register in the old Protestant church at Mallow has an intriguing entry for the funeral service of James Sullivan, 'buried in part. Priests interfered and finished the Service.' These were indeed unecumenical days!

James and Mary had twelve children, ten of whom survived. It was their eighth child, Edward, who established a thriving wine-merchant business in Mallow. He also acquired considerable property, purchasing part of the Castle Hyde estate in Fermoy and elsewhere in West Cork. Towards the end of his life he retired to Dublin, where he lived at 11 Raglan Road. He died in 1867 (when his grandson John would have been six years of age).

Edward and Anne Sullivan had four children. Their eldest son, Edward, (the future Lord Chancellor of Ireland and father of Father John) was born in 1822 in Mallow. He was educated at Midleton School in County Cork and later at Trinity College, where he graduated in 1845 with great distinction.

He was called to the Irish Bar and began an illustrious legal career which was to be crowned with success. In 1860 he was appointed Third Sergeant, in 1861 Bencher of the Kings' Inns and Second Sergeant, in 1865 Solicitor-General, in 1868 Attorney General, and then Master of the Rolls, and finally in 1883 he became Lord Chancellor of Ireland. In 1881 he was created baronet.

Sir Edward Sullivan was known as a firm judge who delivered many memorable judgements at a time of great political upheaval in Ireland. He was also a member of parliament for Mallow, elected on behalf of the Liberal Party in 1865 and in 1868. He played a leading role in the disestablishment of the Church of Ireland in 1869-1871 and entertained the British prime minister, W.E. Gladstone, at his residence at 32 Fitzwilliam Place. Here, the eight-year-old youngest child of the Sullivan family, John, may well have heard conversations between his father and the Grand Old Man of the Liberal Party.

Sir Edward died suddenly on 13 April 1885. On the previous evening he had dined in the company of the Prince and Princess of Wales at the Vice-Regal Lodge in the Phoenix Park, sitting next to Princess Alexandra. During the course of the evening he took ill and returned to his home in Fitzwilliam Place, where he died the following day.

John Sullivan was born on 8 May 1861 at 41 Eccles Street in the heart of old Georgian Dublin. The house is situated opposite the hall door of the old Mater Nursing Home. The street sweeps down to the magnificent perspective of St George's Church, where John was baptised on 15 July 1861 by the Reverend David Stewart, the curate of St Georges. It was soon after this that Edward and Bessie Josephine Sullivan moved with their family to the south side of Dublin – 32 Fitzwilliam Place, which was to be home to the Sullivans for over forty years. John had three older brothers. Edward was born in 1852, and was destined to be a very distinguished literary figure and a famed bibliophile. His name is still associated with the first studio edition of the Book of Kells, which was first published in 1914 and has been reprinted in recent years. He was well acquainted with the writings of Goethe, Dante and other great figures of European literature. His translation of Dante's *Divine Comedy*, which he gave as a gift to his younger brother John, is on display in the People's Church at Clongowes.

On his father's death, Edward became the second baronet. Robert, the second son, died in a tragic drowning accident in Killiney near the Sullivan home, Undercliff, in 1877. He was twenty-three years of age.

The third son, William, became the third and last baronet on his brother Edward's death in the early 1930s. William and John were close to each other. It was Sir William who was with John when he died, and he declared at that time, 'He was the best brother a man could have'.

In those days preceding the 'Ne Temere' decree, the boys of the Sullivan family were brought up in the Protestant tradition of their father, and the only daughter, Annie, was brought up in the Catholic tradition of their mother. From his earliest years, John enjoyed the great benefits of a home that radiated warm affection, high culture, and sound scholarship.

Father John Sullivan SJ.

In 1873 John and his brother William were sent to Portora Royal School, Enniskillen, following in the footsteps of the older brothers Edward and Robert. The headmaster of Portora was one of the outstanding educationalists of the time, Dr William Steele. John's years in Portora were happy. In one of the few writings which he had published (the foreword to the biography of John Haughton Steele, son of Dr Steele who, like John, became a Catholic priest), he admits that he went to Portora for the first time 'bathed in tears' but when the time came to leave he wept 'more plentiful tears'! John remembered Portora with affection, and Portora remembers him. Today his name is inscribed, for all to see, on the Royal Scholars Honours Board in Steele Hall at Portora.

Contemporaries of the young John Sullivan recall him as a popular boy who was always gentle and kind, especially to new boys who found the new life in boarding school difficult — he probably remembered his own beginnings there. Portora and its surroundings made a deep impression on John. Devenish Island, with its ruined Round Tower, steeped in early Irish history of the monastic period, must have stirred him deeply — as it did many generations of Portorans. Maybe it was here that he experienced the first movements of spiritual awakening.

After Portora John went to Trinity. Unlike his father and his brothers, he does not seem to have been an active member of the many societies that flourished in Trinity at this time. But he did distinguish himself in his studies, and in 1883 was awarded the Gold Medal in Classics (which is now carefully preserved at Clongowes). After achieving a Senior Moderatorship in Classics, John started to study Law. It was at this time that his father died, and the shock had a devastating effect. The promising young scholar left Ireland and continued his studies at Lincoln's Inn, London where he was called to the Bar in 1888. At this time, due to his inheritance, he was very comfortable in financial terms, noted for his fashionable dress and handsome good looks. He travelled a great deal and was a great cycling enthusiast.

We are now at a period when very little is known of his inner feelings and struggle. Like many young adults he probably set out on the marvellous adventure of life, not very sure of where he was going but in an intense spirit of search and exploration. There must have been the times of uncertainty – but he continued to search. Then, in December 1896, at the age of thirty-five, he made the momentous decision – he decided to become a Catholic. He was received into the Catholic Church in the Jesuit church in Farm Street, London.

The family were shell-shocked when the news reached Dublin, according to Sir William's granddaughter, Mrs Nedda Davis, who remembers her grandfather talking of the affair. Not that the family members were in any way hostile to John's decision; after all, John's mother, whom he adored, was a devout Catholic. It was simply that John had never expressed any great interest in theological matters and seemed to be such a 'typical Protestant' of the best possible mould! We can imagine the reaction of Lady Sullivan on receiving the news. It was probably an answer to her prayers. She died two years later, in 1898.

Having recovered from the news of John's conversion to Catholicism, the family received a further shock. He decided to become a priest, and to enter the Society of Jesus. The year was 1900. His training as a Jesuit followed the usual pattern. The programme of formation, which began with the first two years of the noviciate at Tullabeg, was followed by studies in Philosophy and Theology. But from the beginning he was so different from everyone else. To his new way of life, he gave himself completely. All who lived with him could not fail to notice his dedication to prayer and to the demands of religious life. Despite his outstanding intellectual gifts he never paraded his knowledge, but was always careful to help others whenever possible.

He was ordained at Milltown Park on Sunday 28 July 1907, and was then sent to Clongowes to begin a life of pastoral service, which continued until his death in 1933. For the period between 1919 and 1924, Father John was rector of Rathfarnham Castle. Apart from this time his life as a Jesuit priest was based in Clongowes.

In the solitude of the beautiful surroundings of Clongowes, John must have remembered earlier times at Portora and Devenish Island. In the companionship of silence and solitude and in the quiet of his prayer he listened to God – and found Him. In that stillness and peace he obviously found the nourishment that gave him inner strength, and in the afterglow of his prayer he brought God to others.

Many of the boys in Clongowes who were taught by him remember him as someone who was very different and special. He was a good counsellor – but a bad teacher! The boys often considered that they passed their exams more through the power of his prayers than the quality of his teaching, despite his brilliant mind and intellectual achievement. The brilliant scholar is not always the best teacher, but a holy man is always a holy man. And the power of that holiness was recognised. For many of his former pupils it was only in later years that they realised how extraordinary it was 'to be taught by a saint'.

Father John was known far beyond the confines of Clongowes. He was a constant friend to the poor and to anyone who was in any need or distress. His reputation for holiness and for the strange gift of healing, of the body as of the spirit, brought many seeking his help and encouragement – and his prayers worked! The stories of his cures are legion, although Father John would have been appalled at any effort to imply that he had cured anybody. Quite rightly, he always attributed such extraordinary healing to the power of prayer, and he always insisted that it was not his achievement nor his influence – but his many friends recognised 'the power of God working in him'. John had the sort of faith that gave him the right sort of confidence. His deep faith, his prayer and his determination won results over and over again, but without any hint of triumphalism.

Around Clane there are many families who treasure the records of the past, records of how Father John brought healing and peace to troubled lives. In his biography of Father John, Father Fergal McGrath wrote the following:

> There were instances in which Fr. Sullivan seemed to secure for sick persons the gift of freedom from physical pain or mental suffering, even though a cure did not follow. About 1913 Fr. Sullivan was asked by Mr Peter Coonan, a near neighbour of Clongowes, to visit his uncle, Thomas Coonan, who was dying of bleeding cancer of the throat at his home, Kilclough, near Straffan, County Kildare. Mr Peter Coonan drove Fr. Sullivan over in his gig, and when they got near the house they could hear the sick man moaning and crying out in a most distressing way. Fr. Sullivan prayed over him for a considerable time. He then rose to go and said, 'Good-bye, Tom, and I promise you one thing, that you won't suffer any more'. Thomas Coonan died about a fortnight later and never suffered any pain after Fr. Sullivan's visit. The extraordinary change in his condition was a subject of comment by many neighbours, still living, who visited him.

Early in February 1927 the wife of Mr Laurence J. Fullam, Assistant County Surveyor, County Kildare, was dangerously ill. This is her husband's story:

> My wife was dying of double pneumonia. She had passed through one crisis, and, when the second came, the two doctors who were in attendance told me that very little hope could be entertained for her recovery. She was almost continually unconscious and had been kept alive for two or three days by oxygen. When I heard what the doctors had to say, I suggested getting a specialist from Dublin. On his arrival, the three doctors held a consultation. They then called me into the room and the specialist acted as spokesman. He told me that, though they, as doctors, must keep fighting as long as there was the slightest hope, his own opinion was that it was now only a matter of a few hours.
> Without telling anybody where I was going, I rushed off in my car at full speed to get Fr. Sullivan. I met him in the College grounds. Without waiting to get hat or coat, although it was winter time, he came with me. Coming along I said to him 'Father, if ever you worked a miracle, you must work one in this case for the mother of eight small children.' His only answer was to start humming a hymn. When we arrived at the house, he prayed for about half an hour over my wife, who was then completely unconscious. On our way back, he called to Clane convent to ask the prayers of the nuns, and also made a visit to the Blessed Sacrament in the parish church. Before we parted, he told me to put my trust in God and that my wife

would recover. Next morning she was so much improved that I rushed out to send off telegrams to friends and relatives to say that she was out of danger. The improvement continued daily. She was up in about three weeks' time and was able to travel to Dublin on the following St. Patrick's Day.

In 1928 occurred the cure of Micheál Collins, a nephew of the famous political leader Michael Collins, and then a little child of three. His parents, Mr and Mrs Seán Collins, were then living in Celbridge, County Kildare. Up to that time the child had been in perfect health. Very early on the morning of Monday 8 October 1928 the parents were woken by violent screams. On running into the room where the boy was sleeping, they found his right leg twisted upward and inward so that the foot was almost touching the chest. He was in great agony and when they tried to straighten the leg he cried piteously. The local doctor, Dr Charles O'Connor, was summoned at once, and after careful examination declared that he feared it was a case of infantile paralysis. Mrs Collins said that she would prefer that the child should die than live a cripple, and Dr O'Connor replied, 'I am glad you realise how serious it is'. The next day a well-known Dublin surgeon was called into consultation. He held out very little hope but advised that the child should be removed to the Mater Hospital, Dublin.

On the following morning, before breakfast, Mr Collins was standing on the road outside his house when two woodmen named Byrne happened to pass. They had often seen the little boy with his father and, missing him, enquired where he was. When Mr Collins told them of the child's illness they at once urged that the child should be brought over to Father Sullivan in Clongowes. They spoke with such conviction about the holiness of Father Sullivan, and about the cures attributed to him, that Mr Collins, who had never heard of him before, was deeply impressed. He went in to inform his wife of the conversation and she replied that she was just about to speak to him on the same subject, as their chauffeur had come in to advise her to bring the child over to Father Sullivan. They were afraid to bring the child so far, but Mrs Collins herself drove over to Clongowes. Father Sullivan came down to the hall to see her, and her first reaction was disappointment. He kept his eyes fixed on the ground, said very little, and did not seem to be much interested in the matter. However, when she was coming away he said, 'do not worry,' and promised to say Mass for the child next morning.

That evening the child was brought to the Mater hospital and left in the children's ward. After an X-ray the surgeon explained that he did not think there was any chance of the child making a recovery. On the following four days various members of the family visited him and found no change. However, on Tuesday morning, 16 October, Mrs Collins received a postcard from Father Sullivan that she has treasured ever since. It read as follows:

Dublin 5pm
15.X.28.

I have just seen Micheál & delighted to hear he was going home well.

Yours etc.
John Sullivan, SJ

Mrs Collins had heard nothing of this sudden improvement. She immediately hurried out to catch the first bus to Dublin, and on arriving at the hospital, met the sister in charge who told her that the child was indeed cured. The evening before, Father Sullivan had arrived on his bicycle from Clongowes (it should be noted that he was then sixty-six). He prayed for a long time over the child and touched his leg. When he had gone, the nun thought the child looked better, took him out of bed and put him into a warm bath. He immediately kicked out quite normally with the leg that had hitherto been useless. He was brought home the next day; never had the slightest trouble afterwards, and indeed grew up particularly strong and well, distinguishing himself in the world of schoolboy swimming.

In 1929 John Nevin, who lived at Betaghstown, near Clongowes, was dying of cancer of the face. The malady had worked terrible ravages, almost entirely destroying one side of the face. The doctor who attended the case recalled it as one of the worst he had known and found it difficult himself to approach the patient. During the last five weeks of this man's life, Father Sullivan would visit him every day, and during the last fortnight twice a day. He would kneel beside his bed for a considerable time, and the doctor recalled his amazement at seeing Father Sullivan leaning right over the sufferer, with his face almost touching the patient's. A relative was struck by the fact that Father Sullivan seemed to have no fear of the cancer, and would put his arms round the poor man in his bed. The list of cures and events goes on.

The Father Sullivan memorial at the abbey, Clane.

The years at Clongowes are a record of spiritual testimony. In a time of political upheaval in Ireland, nothing is known of Father John's political views. His physical appearance and style of dress belied the fashionable young man of the end of the nineteenth century he had been. The stylish dress of his earlier years was gone forever. He now wore the worn, patched clothing of the very poor. He identified with the poorest of the poor, and lived a very rugged, ascetic life. His meals were very simple: he lived mainly on dry bread, porridge, rice, and cold tea. He slept little, spending most of the night in prayer. His room at Clongowes lacked even the very simple comforts of the day. The fire, in the winter, was lit only when he was expecting a visitor. His lifestyle reflected the hardship and simplicities of the early Desert Fathers – a life of austerity and prayer. Until the time of his death he was in demand as a preacher at retreats for religious communities of men and women. These again were an experience of his holiness rather than his eloquence.

One interest from the past that he maintained was his interest in cycling – his old-fashioned bicycle was a familiar sight around the roads of Clane. He was known to have cycled to Dublin on more than one occasion in order to visit the sick, and having prayed with the sick person he would then set out immediately on the return journey. His passion for what was, in his early days, a new-fangled invention, stood him in good stead in his later years. When not travelling by bicycle, he usually walked.

Father John's reputation as a saint grew rapidly during his time at Clongowes. Very few knew of his family history, or of the fashionable young man-about-town, which formed a stark contrast with the poor man who was their priest and friend.

In the weeks before his death, Father John became increasingly ill. In early February he asked to see the doctor – a most unusual request from him – about a swelling in his arm. His final days in Clongowes were spent in the infirmary, where he was cared for by the matron. On Friday 17 February his condition deteriorated considerably. He was in intense pain when he was removed to St Vincent's Nursing Home, where he underwent immediate surgery. After the operation it was clear that his condition was hopeless, and although he suffered less he began to sink rapidly. Throughout the Saturday and Sunday, although he was conscious, he was clearly dying. He received Holy Communion on both days and was remarkably resigned to God's Will and seemed to experience great peace. He tried to join in the prayers that were said at his bedside and when he was asked how he felt, replied: 'Wonderfully well, thank God'. All who assisted him in his final days marvelled at his deep faith in God, his patience, and his obedience.

When the end seemed to be drawing near, the rector, Father George Roche, asked him if he wished to send a message to the boys at Clongowes, and he managed to whisper 'God bless and protect them'.

His only surviving brother, Sir William Sullivan, was with him as the end approached. Sir William, on hearing of Father John's illness, had travelled immediately from his home in England. He was at his brother's bedside when, at 10.55p.m. on Sunday 19 February 1933, Father John breathed his last.

Great crowds gathered for the funeral Mass to bid a farewell to their beloved priest. The Bishop of Kildare and Leighlin, Dr Cullen, presided at the Office and Solemn Requiem Mass and later said the prayers at the graveside when Father John was laid to rest in the community cemetery.

Father Sullivan's funeral mass, Clongowes Wood chapel.

Father Sullivan's coffin being carried from Clongowes Wood chapel for burial.

For many it was difficult to imagine Clongowes without the stooped, shuffling figure who was such a familiar sight around the place. He had become a deep-rooted presence in so many lives that it was presumed that he would always be there 'up at the College'.

During his lifetime and even more so after his death, many believed in Father John's holiness with a deeply-held conviction. His grave became a place of pilgrimage, and there was a constant demand for keepsakes and items of his clothing, which were treasured as relics.

In 1947 it was decided to propose Father John as a candidate for canonisation. As a result of the initial inquiry, Father John was declared Servant of God in 1960. His mortal remains were removed from the Jesuit cemetery at Clongowes and brought to a special tomb in the Sacred Heart Chapel in St Francis Xavier's Church in Dublin. Every day, people come to pray and to seek the support of his prayers.

Much has happened in recent years. At a special Mass of Thanksgiving to mark the fiftieth anniversary of Father John's death, the late Dr Patrick Lennon, Bishop of Kildare and Leighlin, came to Clongowes to pay tribute to the Servant of God. In his address he noted that while we must wait patiently for the formal judgement of the Holy See in matters of canonisation, in his opinion Father John has already passed the most difficult of all tribunals – the judgement of the schoolboys of his day who recognised his sanctity. Schoolboys, Bishop Lennon declared, are severe in their judgement of anything that is false or a sham.

T.J. Garrett, a former headmaster of Portora Royal School, Enniskillen, noted in his foreword to Father Edward Keelaghan's short biography of Father John Sullivan:

> John Sullivan's splendid academic record at Portora is itself a testimony to the enormous interest which Dr. Steele must have taken in the young boy from Dublin, and I like to think that the influence of Dr. Steele also stood by the young Jesuit Father Sullivan as he embarked upon his own teaching career at that other great Irish school, Clongowes Wood College; and in later years too, as his life increasingly exemplified the highest Christian virtues, the simple precepts instilled into the boy during his years at Portora may well have sustained him in his constant devotion to Christ.

Since then Clongowes and Portora have shared a bond in memory of the distinguished past pupil of Portora and the holy priest of Clongowes.

Another remarkable recent event has been the very welcome and enthusiastic support of the Church of Ireland in various ceremonies honouring this extraordinary Jesuit. It is not forgotten that Father John was a member of the Church of Ireland until the age of thirty. One of his great admirers was the late Archbishop George Otto Simms. When asked why he was so enthusiastic about Father John being honoured by the Church of Rome, he responded that we must remember that John was a member of the Church of Ireland into mature adulthood. By then his character would already have been well-formed. Through his holiness he would have learnt in the Anglican tradition and the Roman Catholic Church then reaped the benefits of that solid foundation!

Dr Simms agreed to give the address when some members of the Church of Ireland proposed to celebrate a memorial service to honour Father John's life and work. The Service of Worship took place on 8 May 1983 in St George's Church, Temple Street, Dublin, where John was baptised. Bishop James Kavanagh attended, representing the Catholic Archdiocese of Dublin. He delivered a special message of greeting from Pope John Paul II. The text read:

Father Sullivan's grave at Clongowes, 1933.

Transfer of remains of Fr John Sullivan, Staplestown. Following the hearse, Mollie Delaney and son Nickey, Kathleen Ward and Maureen Casey.

Città Vaticano

Bishop Kavanagh,
Archbishop's House,
Dublin.

I am informed that you will participate in the Ecumenical Service of Thanksgiving commemorating the fiftieth anniversary of the death of Father John Sullivan.

His Holiness asks you to convey his cordial greetings to all present.

In communion of prayer he gives thanks to Almighty God for the extraordinary gifts bestowed on Father Sullivan during his life and for the spirit of mutual understanding, reconciliation and goodwill which his memory enkindles between various Christian communities in Ireland today.

His Holiness prays that this Service in St George's Church where Father Sullivan was first joined to Christ in Baptism will bring spiritual joy and comfort to you all.

Cardinal Casorali.

In his address Archbishop Simms stressed how much Christian communities have in common, sharing many hallowed traditions, and how this particular occasion resonated with a jubilee ring for this 'native of St George's Parish'. In a thought-provoking sermon, Dr Simms supplied thoroughly researched biographical background to Father John's life as an Anglican leading up to 'when he found his spiritual home in the Jesuit Church at Farm Street, London'.

There have been other memorial services celebrated according to the Anglican rite since that first memorable occasion. Among the eminent figures of the Church of Ireland who have preached at these ceremonies are Archbishop G.O. Simms, Archbishop Walton Empey, Archbishop Donald Caird, Canon Adrian Empey and Dean Maurice Carey. All have contributed beautifully to honouring this outstanding Jesuit who was a spiritual son of the Church of Ireland.

The life of Father John Sullivan sets an example for all who seek God. It is the story of a most extraordinary pilgrimage. One old woman whom he had helped perhaps provides the key to who this extraordinary man was; 'Father Sullivan is very hard on himself'.

Clane still remembers Father John with pride and affection. Clane Community Council erected a monument in his memory in the village, and this memorial has since been moved to the grounds of the old abbey where, on Saturday, 16 October 1999, it was re-dedicated by Most Reverend Laurence Ryan, Bishop of Kildare and Leighlin. The people of Mainham honour his memory with a handsome monument and garden of remembrance at Mainham cemetery.

In 2001 the Supplementary Tribunal of Enquiry, set up by the Archbishop of Dublin, sent its findings to the Holy See in Rome. The cause for his beatification continues.

Many of Father John's friends in Clane hope and pray that one day he will be declared a saint. God grant that it may be soon.

VI

JIMMY REDDY, POSTMAN
(1882-1956)

John Noonan

My grandfather, Jimmy Reddy, delivered the post for over fifty years around Clane. He was born on 24 April 1882 in a house opposite what is now McKenna's hardware shop on the Dublin road. His parents were Larry Reddy from Capdoo and Mary Whelan from Kilkenny. Both Larry and Mary worked in McCrackens's Textile Mill at the Liffey bridge. They fell in love and married on 29 June 1881. They had three sons and one daughter.

Jimmy went to school in Clane. In later years, he often recited a rhyme the pupils were required to learn every Shrove Tuesday. It went like this:

> Oh teacher, Oh teacher,
> Be faithful and kind,
> And don't let the pancakes
> Go out of your mind
>
> When you were a schoolboy,
> You liked to be free
> So give us a half-day
> And we'll be thankful to thee.

Jimmy's first and only full-time job was as postman. The postmistress at the time was Theresa O'Neill. The O'Neills also had a pub and grocery shop attached to the post office. Christy McCormack also delivered the post. He was known as the walking postman because he delivered the post on foot, whereas Jimmy made his deliveries on a bike. Christy also had the nickname 'the waterhen' because of his long legs, and he walked up to twenty miles a day.

But Jimmy also worked part-time as a handyman and did a lot of work for the convent and the priests. He was known as the best handyman in Clane, and to this day, examples of his work can be seen in the village. He built the piers for the gates at Abbeylands for the O'Neills in 1934 – they can still be seen on the Clane-Sallins road.

Jimmy married Esther McCormack from Moat Commons. They had five daughters, two of whom died young. Esther died in her early forties, leaving Jimmy with three children to rear. My mother, Mona, then aged twelve, was the eldest. She took over the household duties and looked after her two little sisters, the youngest only two years old at the time. It was not easy as there was no running water or electricity then. Mona had to walk half a mile for drinking water and cross a field to a nearby spring just to get water for washing. Cooking was over an open fire.

Jimmy sowed a half-acre garden in vegetables to feed his family. They also ate a lot of fish caught by him in the Liffey. The big treat was stuffed rabbit for Sunday dinner. The house that Jimmy and his family lived in on the Millicent road was built around 1890, and was known as a Parnell house. I, his grandson, still live in that very same house.

Sport played a major part in Jimmy's life: two world champions came from Clane – Tommy Conneff was a runner and Jack Dempsey a boxer. Clane GAA grounds are called after Tommy Conneff. Jack Dempsey's real name was John Edward Kelly. He lived with his family on the back avenue of Clongowes Wood College, and to the present day, where he lived is still known as Kelly's farm. He was middleweight champion of the world, and some boxing historians still consider him the best pound-for-pound boxer of all time. Both men trained in the field opposite the John Sullivan Centre, which is still simply known as the sports field by the locals.

Jim Archer of Moat Commons was one of the founders of Clane GAA club. He was the first man to have fifteen men on a team. Before that, teams had twenty-one or seventeen players, which made the pitch very crowded. Jim's son, Fred Archer, joined the Free State Army when Michael Collins was commander. He got a bullet in the back of his neck, which was there till the day he died. When he left the army he robbed a pistol and bullets with the intention of assassinating Éamon de Valera. He reckoned Dev was 'the man that got Michael Collins shot'. Fred was a commander of the local IRA during the War of Independence, and took part in ambushes in Kill and Johnstown. He was also involved in the burning of the RIC barracks in the village, now Des Marron's chemist shop.

Jimmy also loved football and hurling. His brother-in-law, Ned McCormack, won twelve senior championship medals with Clane. Half the Kildare team were Clane men at the time, and they won Leinster and All-Ireland medals. Men like Larry Hussey Cribbin, Steel Losty, the Brackens and Mick Sammon were household names. Mick Sammon was Jimmy's best friend and an All-Ireland medal winner in 1919. He refereed the match between Tipperary and Dublin on Bloody Sunday in Croke Park. Another great sporting outing for Jimmy was the once-a-year point-to-point race meeting at Windgates on the Straffan-Maynooth road.

Jimmy also played pitch and toss at Hogan's corner, now called Manzor's. Another pastime was going to the Forge at night. This was situated at the triangle on the Naas side of Clane. Geoghegan's had a public house and a butcher's stall at that end of Clane. There were also two pubs at the other side of the village; one owned by McKittricks (now Manzor's), and Daly's (now Manzor's gift shop). There was a water pump opposite McKittrick's and Jimmy said many times that anyone who drank out of McKittrick's pump never left Clane.

Jimmy was rarely outfaced by anyone. At the time, Abbeylands, the house lived in until recently by Charlie O'Neill, was owned by a Mr Penneran, a magistrate. Mr Penneran had a reputation as a harsh man, who horsewhipped anyone found trespassing on his avenue. One day, when Jimmy was delivering the post there, he was accosted by Penneran who asked Jimmy if he realised who he, Penneran was, and if he did, why he didn't salute him. 'I never will', Jimmy replied. 'There's only two people I salute in the village and it's not for who they are, but for what they represent. They are the priest and the Church of Ireland minister. I'll be fecked if I ever salute you.'

Our postman Jimmy Reddy.

Fred and Mick Archer were Jimmy's close neighbours. They were hay-mongers, and in summer they delivered hay to Smithfield market in Dublin, leaving Clane in the early hours of the morning. Their nephew, Jack Cullen, who lived with them, often recalled how he would wake up at 5a.m. and hear Fred encouraging his horse. 'Come on Ned' he'd say, 'I want to bring you to Dublin to show you a double-decker bus.' On the way, the brothers would stop off at Lucan with their two drays. At Ball Alley they would get feed for the horses and sleep for an hour or two under the drays. To get up the steep hill at Lucan they had to hitch the two horses to one dray, unhitch them at the top, and come back for the other dray. Coming home in darkness with their hay sold, they dreaded coming through Lucan because they might be stopped by the guard if they had no lights. Mostly they simply lit up for the journey through the town, then put out their candles once they were out in the country again. Then they would snuggle down in one of the drays under what hay was left and sleep while the horses made their own way home.

There were two lodging houses in Clane at the time, Aggie Weir's and Walsh's. They were situated in the place now occupied by Campbell's Tyre Centre. It was said it cost 6d for a bed without fleas and 3d with fleas – mostly tramps lodged there. One of them was a Patrick O'Connor, who on the night of 3 March 1923, when he was lodging in Walsh's, was arrested for robbing a coat belonging to Elizabeth Coffey. At Drumcondra court he was asked by the judge why he took the coat and replied 'Because I wanted it'. The judge said 'Fair enough' and let him off. On 3 March 1923 the Garda Barracks in Clane was attacked by five armed men. Five bikes and four overcoats were stolen.

The year of 1949 was a year to remember in Clane: it was the year Clane team won the Intermediate Football Championship. Jimmy's son-in-law, big Joe Noonan, was captain of the team. There was also a murder committed in the area that year. A man went missing in August, but his body was not found until December, when it was discovered in a potato pit. Jimmy's next-door neighbour, James Harrington, was killed by a train on the track at Newbridge station, leaving behind a young wife and a family of ten.

Retiring age at that time was seventy. Although Jimmy had an enlarged heart and other health problems, Dr Walsh did not have the heart to pension him off. Jimmy's own attitude was 'I'll wear out but I'll not rust out'. He kept going until he could go no longer. He delivered the post in Clane for fifty-two years.

VII

THE LAIDBACK FIFTIES TO THE DANCING SIXTIES

Paddy Behan

Growing up in the fifties, times were hard and money was scarce. I guess that what I have just said was uttered by every generation before me going back hundreds of years. Money was scarce for most families but one thing we were never short of was love – the love of a great mother and father, the love between brothers and sisters, the loving kindness of wonderful grandparents, aunts and uncles and great neighbours. This meant we were happy most of the time and any little extra was a bonus.

Entertainment started for me when I was about four years old. I can still hear the sound made by the wheels of the pram as my father, Pat Behan, pushed it back and forth singing 'The Stone Outside Dan Murphy's Door', 'The Star of the County Down' and 'Sweet Rosie O'Grady'. As my father was a nice singer it generally had the desired effect and my baby brother or sister eventually went to sleep. During all this I was tucked up warm in bed and to this day I still remember the words of the above songs.

My next form of entertainment was a few years later and was provided by my life-long friend and co-author Bryan Sammon. Bryan then lived where the bungalows are built in Loughbollard. His father, Tommy, had a nice house and land there. Tommy was a great man, full of kindness and patience. He erected a stage in his garage, complete with a white sheet which acted as a curtain. Bryan, even at that early age, was already a leader, and he wrote two plays: *Noddy* and *Aladdin*. We had many happy days there and to us it was as good as the Gaiety in Dublin! Bryan's mother, Ellen, would come out at the end of the play with glasses of orange and biscuits, which was a big treat in those days.

My first introduction to public entertainment would have been the variety concerts in Clane hall. These concerts would consist of three one-act comedies, reels and jigs by some local girls, and music provided on the accordion and violin by men from Clane. I remember in particular the late Patsy Dunne, from St Brigid's Terrace, a great neighbour and a great musician. There was always a raffle at these concerts and one night my Granny Lavin, an aunt of the great Pa Connolly, bought 2s' worth of tickets. She gave me half of them and I was lucky enough to win the prize of a 10s note – fifty cent today would be the equivalent. It kept me in bull's-eyes, Lemon Drops, Acid Drops, and Flash Bars for weeks.

A much bigger and more professional concert was held every year in the fifties at Clongowes Wood College. It was promoted by Clane Gaelic Football Club and drew a large and appreciative audience. People came from miles around, even from Newbridge and Naas. The Clane Drama Group put on a three-act play every year: *Shadow of a Gunman, Juno and*

Clane 1941: Maureen Harrington, Kathy Reddy, Jo Reddy, Tom Behan, Mary McConnell, Georgie Harrington, Betty Harrington, Christie Campbell and Kitty McIntyre.

the Paycock, *The New Gossoon*, and many more. I can remember my father, Del Weld, Seán Cribbin, Christy Brien, Carmel Marron, Eileen Tiernan, Danny Smyth, Josie Doyle and Mick Dunne from Blackhall – they were brilliant actors and could have held their own in the Abbey Theatre. Mike Nolan was the compère of the last concert I attended there. Kevin Hilton was another great compère. We all loved Charlie Byrne with his 'Kojak' bald head. Monica Bonnie was a beautiful xylophone player. Albert Healy played the accordion and was very popular. I remember a fine West Indian singer by the name of Othmar Remy Arthur – he was a favourite with the audience. The poor man was killed in a road accident in Kildare town a few years later. Rev. Father Hughes who was CC in Clane at that time in the fifties put a lot of work into running the concerts and everyone loved him. I remember one incident from the Clongowes concerts very vividly, it was around 1954 – I was seven years old then. The front two rows of seats were reserved for the Jesuit priests and brothers. I was sitting in the front row between two Jesuit priests, when my father, acting in *Shadow of a Gunman*, was shot. I jumped up immediately and began to cry – the Jesuit priest tried to calm me down.

Patrick and Brigid Behan –
Paddy Behan's parents, 1945.

explaining that it was only make-believe but I was not convinced, so he took me backstage.
You can imagine my delight when I saw my father there, very much alive with a cup of tea
in one hand and a sandwich in the other.

The next milestone on my entertainment journey was when my grandfather, Paddy Lavin,
who had a shop in Clane where the Spar shop is today, went to Dublin to buy a radio for us in
1957. We waited anxiously until he came up to our house in St Brigid's Terrace and installed the
radio. It was brown in colour and made by Bush. My father had made a shelf about five feet up
on the wall and had also put up an eighteen-foot-long steel pole outside the house to act as an
aerial. We waited with baited breath until Granddad switched on the radio – it worked perfectly
and the reception was great. We got years of enjoyment from that little radio, listening to the
one and only Mícheál Ó Hehir commentating on the various football matches in the fifties and
sixties. My father loved the Irish songs, so we never missed 'Chéile House' on a Saturday night.
I also remember the many sponsored programmes, like 'Donnelly Sausages', 'Urney Chocolates'
and 'Waltons' ('If you feel like singing do sing an Irish song – the songs our fathers loved').

CLANE G.F.C. DRAMATIC CLUB
will hold their first

ANNUAL DANCE
in
CLANE HALL
On Sunday, May 14th
Music by Gallowglass Band.
Dancing: 9 - 3.
ADMISSION 3/6
Refreshments (extra) by P. Lavin.
(1950)   1287z1

The Clane G.F.C. annual dance, 1950.

Probably the biggest breakthrough in entertainment came around 1958, when one of my friends, Robbie Booth, got a record player as a present from his aunt in Dublin. The first record I ever heard played live was by an Australian, Slim Dusty, singing 'The Pub With No Beer'. We spent many happy hours down in Booth's house playing records – I don't know how Molly Booth put up with the noise. But like her husband, Dick, she never complained and they always welcomed us into their house.

Another example of a patient woman was my Aunt Statia. She lived in the house beside ours and got a television before we did. My brothers and myself went in to her on many occasions and saw programmes like *The Aquanauts*, *Get Smart*, *Hawaii Five-O*, and many others.

As we got a bit older, say around twelve, we used to hang around outside the hall in Clane. I remember Christy Connolly's céile band playing there. They were fantastic and drew big crowds. Christy later married a local girl, Josie Doyle, sister of Patti McCormack. After hearing Christy's band we all wanted to be musicians. Some learned the accordion, some the drums – I wanted to learn the guitar. Father Tom O'Malley CC, Clane, tried his best to teach me to play the guitar, but he did not succeed. I had no patience – some would say, 'what's new?'

The Table Tennis Club in Clane was going strong in those years, thanks to the work of many committed members. One member in particular stands out and that was Peter Duffy. He kept

The Calandos. Back row: Percy Jones, Paddy Blanch, Mick Lawlor, Peter Gordon. Front row: Dermot Byrne, John Egan, Jimmy Kelly.

the club going in good times and in bad, and was always available to drive teams to matches in Dublin, Abbeyleix, Enniscorthy and many other places. The highlight of our life at that time was the Table Tennis Christmas Party, which was held in January in the hall. Tickets would be printed and each member would get six tickets to sell. They sold like hot cakes – they sold out quicker than U2 or Eminem, mainly because the band playing at the party were our pride and joy – local band The Calandos. Now don't get me wrong, we loved the Rolling Stones, the Beatles, the Beach Boys and the Kinks, but to see a band live on stage, no group could compare to them. I remember John Egan, the drummer, nicknamed 'Paladin', because he looked very like a fine American actor who featured on a cowboy series called 'Have Gun Will Travel'. John was a great drummer and many said he could make the drums talk. Percy Jones was the 'cool dude' who played the saxophone. The crowd just stood in amazement at the great sounds Percy got from his beautiful shining sax. Mick Lawlor was the leader of the band and played sax. He was a Billy Fury look-alike and could sing every bit as good as Billy Fury. Paddy Blanche played trumpet, Jimmy Kelly played bass guitar, Dermot Byrne played lead guitar and was lead vocalist, and Peter Gordon played the slide trombone. I would like to thank Mick, John, Percy and the rest of the band for the many fantastic hours of music they gave to us. Some of the lads are still playing today and maybe The Calandos might consider reforming – that would really be something.

CYMS. hall in Rathcoffey in 1952. Back row: Molly Murray, Elizabeth Gill (now Lee), Kitty ? (now Reid), Eileen Reilly, Joan O'Connor (later Flanagan). Front row: Bernadette O'Brien (now Mullally), Mary Travers (now O'Connell), Mrs Coonan, Miss Byrne, Ciss Brilly, Sally White, Evelyn de Courcey, Mrs Merriman, Sarah O'Neill.

The carnivals also provided many happy hours for us. The carnival in Clane was held in Manzor's Field, the old football field, where Loughbollard Estate is now. It consisted of swinging boats, a wheel of fortune, a pogo tent and a putting green. Our favourite was the swinging boats. At the end of the evening the four swinging boats were pushed up high and a long heavy wooden beam was put in place to keep the boats out of reach. One day, while playing football in Manzor's Field, my co-author Liam Burke, Jim Mahoney, Robbie Booth, Thomas Mahony and my brother Frank decided to try to free the swinging boats. We had to push the boats up a bit to take their weight off the wooden beam. This enabled us to push the beam away from the first boat. We had a great time swinging away for free until Jim Mahoney and myself were in the boat. We were standing up and swinging up very high when suddenly the steel bar of the boat caught the wooden beam, which stopped the boat, dead. We were thrown out onto the ground, but fortunately escaped without injury – we could have been killed so we never tried that again.

There was always a seven-a-side football tournament during the carnival. The prizes were gold watches or suit lengths. I remember the Clane team were in the final. Seamus O'Donnell from Capdoo had a very powerful shot. He soloed in towards the goal and kicked a ferocious

The CYMS. hall in Rathcoffey in 1952. Back row: Mick Berns, John Behan, Tommy Brilly, Michael Behan (Snr), Paddy Reilly, Matt Dunne, Bill Merriman, Jack Kinsella, John Reilly. Front row: Peter Coonan, Jimmy White, Paddy Frayne, Father John Doyle PP, Michael Walsh, Ned O'Neill, Michael Behan.

shot into the goal – the goalkeeper had no chance of saving the shot. Unfortunately, my friend Jim Mahony was standing behind the goals and was hit by the ball. He came close to being the first Irish boy in orbit, but Jim was tough, and after a few minutes he got his wind back and recovered.

Rathcoffey GAA also ran a carnival. Rathcoffey met UCD in the final. UCD were awarded a penalty. Kevin Beahan, a Louth county player, took the penalty. He hit a hard low shot to the corner, but the Rathcoffey keeper, Kit Behan, somehow dived and saved the shot. Everyone said it was the best save ever seen. If we had the money we would go up to Ned and Sarah Neill's shop for an ice-cream. The shop was situated near Painstown Cross. It has now been extended and looks lovely with the beautiful thatched roof. We used to walk to the carnival and always got a lift home from Father John Doyle PP He would pack seven or eight of us into his car.

The Mainliners.

THE SWINGING SIXTIES

Around the mid-sixties we went dancing on Sunday nights to Rathcoffey hall. There were no taxis, so we depended on lifts. Here again we had people like Father Doyle who were very good to us. Two names come to mind – Ollie Reilly of Painstown Pre-cast gave us lifts many times and Larry Higgins, Capdoo, never let us down either. Larry drove a Volkswagen at that time and would cram eight or nine of us into his car. He would never leave any of us on the road and only for him we would have walked home on many occasions.

The dance promoter was a Dublin man named Jimmy Donohue. He used to hire bands mostly from the northern part of the country. One Sunday night he had a band on called Big Tom and the Mainliners – they were very good and when they finished they distributed photos of their band. Liam Burke and I got the band members' autographs on the back of the photo. Jimmy Donohue thanked the band and announced that they would be back soon, but they never returned – the reason being that a month later they had their first number one with a song called 'Gentle Mother'. Their fee for a night went from £60 to £600.

The number one showband in Ireland in the mid-sixties was The Royal Showband from Waterford. My brother-in-law, Robbie Murphy from Naas, was going out with my sister Breda at the time, and they were big fans of the Royal. Breda especially loved Tom Dunphy, the bass player. Robbie would give Liam Burke and myself a lift to Dreamland in Athy. It was a purpose-built ballroom owned by Albert Reynolds (former Taoiseach) and his brother. They had approximately thirteen similar venues around the country like Roseland, Lakeland, and others.

The Big 8.

The Dixies Showband.

Joe Dolan and the Drifters.

We would arrive in Athy around 9.30p.m. Even at that time there would be a large queue outside the main door extending into the car park. We often waited for over an hour before being admitted. I remember St Stephen's night of 1964, when the Royal, as usual, were playing in Dreamland. It was advertised in the *Leinster Leader* at 7/6 admission – 25 cent in today's money. When we eventually reached the main door I was shocked to see a large sign beside the box office showing 'admission 10/='. All I had on me was 10s, so I said to the man in the box office 'you advertised this dance at 7/6'. His reply was 'take it or f—king leave it' – so I paid up.

We did not mind travelling many miles to hear the top showbands. My late father had a Morris 1000, reg. No. BZC 42 and he gave me his car whenever I wanted it. Most of us were pioneers at that time, so my father knew that I would not wreck the car due to drunk driving, but like most young men I was inclined to drive a bit fast.

We went to Edenderry, the home of the Agents Showband, who later became The Fairways. Gary Street was the lead vocalist, Mike Bryan lead guitarist, Pat Cleary was on keyboards, and Ollie Kennedy on guitar. They were a brilliant band and released a few records, which sold very well, like 'Flippidy Flop' and 'Invisible Reilly'. Mick Bryan was a brother of the great Offaly footballer Willie Bryan. Mick was a wonderful guitarist and a lovely guy. Tragically he died in a road accident while coming home from a gig. Another great showband singer and lead guitarist, who died ten years ago, was Liam Gibson. Liam was our age, and when we were nineteen or twenty he came out with us to the dances every weekend. He worked then as a chef in Clongowes Wood College. He was a very friendly chap and got on well with everyone. He played lead guitar with some of the top showbands, including Brian Coll and The Buckaroos. The last time I met Liam was fifteen years ago when The Shadows were

Ballrooms of Romance…   Tom Dunphy.

The Miami Showband.

CLANE YOUTH CLUB

Committee:
B. Sammon,   L. Bourke,
P. Behan,   J. Duffy.

MEMBERSHIP CARD
1965-1966

Name

Kiinsella, Carbury

The Clane Youth Club membership card.

Danny Doyle and Maxie.

Tony McEvoy's house and the Hall, Clane.

playing in the Point in Dublin. Liam was living in Edenderry, married to a beautiful local girl, Bernie. On 11 June 2005 a plaque was unveiled at Edenderry Town Hall commemorating all the deceased musicians from the area. Bryan Sammon and myself went to Edenderry on that very sunny, warm day for the unveiling. A great crowd turned out and everyone enjoyed the music of many showband friends of Liam's, people like Paraic Browne and Jerry McCormack. We met Liam's widow Bernie and had a great chat about the old days.

Another band we loved was known as The Ripchords, later to become The Breakaways, from Naas. The members of this band were Joe Stanley, Paul Flynn, Noel Herterich and Nedser Prendergast. Lawlor's Ballroom in Naas was our favourite venue – all the top bands played there: The Royal, The Dixies, The Drifters, The Miami, Eileen Reid and the Cadets, Big Tom and the Mainliners, and many more. The dances were from 10p.m. to 3a.m. When the Royal Showband played there, a huge crowd came – nearly 3000 packed in. Half of the crowd would just stand and watch Brendan Bowyer jumping around the stage doing his Elvis numbers. Before the Royal went on stage they would always call into Mrs Lawlor's house. She loved the band and they chatted away for an hour or so. Tom Dunphy, the bass guitarist would, coming near the end of their gig, warn everyone about the weather outside. He used to say 'It's snowing outside' or 'It's very frosty, so drive carefully'. Tom was a lovely man and it was ironic that he lost his life in a road accident while driving to a gig in Leitrim in 1975. It was a terrible year, for we also lost members of the Miami Showband. Lead singer Fran O'Toole, trumpeter Brian McCoy and lead guitarist Tony Geraghty were lined up and shot outside Newry by a UVF murder squad. All these great musicians and singers gave so much enjoyment to so many during their short lives – we will never forget them.

Tom Dunphy and Brendan Bowyer had left the Royal in 1972 and formed a new band called The Big 8. Local musician and good friend Billy Hopkins replaced Tom Dunphy on The Royal Showband as bass guitarist. I remember going to Lawlor's, Naas, to hear Billy with The Royal. Billy is still going strong playing at weddings, race meetings, dinner dances, parties, and so on, with his brother Des and Arthur O'Neill. Des Hopkins' son, Graham, is also in the music business and is now regarded as the best rock drummer in the country.

In 1966 Bryan Sammon suggested to Liam Burke, Joe Duffy and myself that we should form a Youth Club. We got Mr Kinsella, a printer from Derrinturn, to design and print the membership cards. As far as I know, I have the only surviving membership card. We approached the GAA committee with a request to hire Clane hall to run Record Hops during the school holidays. We decided that all the profits would go towards holding an Old Folks' Party. Some of the older committee members were not too keen on hops, but with the help of Joe Bracken, Martin Connolly, Seán Cribbin and Ned Coughlan, the committee voted in favour of the hops and charged us £4 per night. This was a fairly high charge, but we accepted it and started to advertise the hops by means of posters in the local shops and by dropping out typed invitations to many houses outside Clane, like Loughanure and Betaghstown. The hops were from 8p.m. to midnight. Admission was 2/6 (10 cent). Bryan obtained a second-hand amplifier for £10 and we purchased a record player on the 'never, never' from Mr Ward of Naas. Jimmy Travers, electrical contractor, from the Straffan road, gave us many speakers from radios, free of charge. The late Mick Reilly, St Brigid's Terrace, made up some wooden cabinets into which we put Jimmy's speakers and we erected these around the hall. The result was fantastic and we were on a high. The crowd loved the sounds of the sixties – their favourite was 'Satisfaction' by the Rolling Stones.

FATHER TOM – A MAN BEFORE HIS TIME

Father Tom O'Malley CC, Clane, did a huge amount of work with us in the Youth Club – he spent a lot of his free time and his money in helping to renovate the interior of the hall. He was a great friend to us all and we will never forget all he did for us. Each day before a hop, the hall had to be cleaned. The big job was cleaning the toilets, especially the men's, but with the help of a can of Jeyes Fluid it turned out ok! After sweeping the dance floor my favourite task was opening a few cans of – no, not Carlsberg – Glideasi. This was thrown across the floor and made it slippery – it was like walking on ice.

At one hop we had a group of forty young lads, sixteen- or seventeen-year-olds from Dublin, who were on a week's holiday in Lonan Murphy House (Millicent House), which was owned or rented at that time by the Society of St Vincent de Paul. There was a religious Brother in charge of the group and we let them in for 2s a head. They were mostly very nice lads, but there was always one who would be out for trouble. One of these lads as he passed the stage pushed it, causing the needle to jump on the record player. I thought it was accidental but when he did it again a few minutes later I followed him down to the men's toilet and told him that if he did not behave he was out. His reply was 'Ok, throw me out' and then he produced a knife about four inches long. I told him to put away the knife or I would report

Reverend Father Tom O'Malley CC, singing 'My Heart Is In Rosario' at Liam Burke's twenty-first birthday party. Margaret Donagher, Billy Burke and Sheila Burke are in the background.

Garda McGuinness, Josie Doyle and Sergeant
Stokes.

Jimmy Dunne.

Eileen Tiernan.

him to Sergeant Egan. His reply was, 'that does not worry me – I have spent many nights in the clink'. This shook me, so I reversed out of the toilet and reported the incident to the Brother in charge of the group. He asked me to point out the lad involved, which I did. The Brother called him over and asked him if he had a knife. The lad reluctantly admitted that he had one, and the Brother said, 'Ok, hand it over', which he did. The Brother then said, 'now you, walk back to Millicent House'. By the look on the lad's face, he clearly did not relish walking two miles along a dark County Kildare road.

Another memory I have of the hops is the Ladies' Choice. We would have two dances during the night when a girl was free to ask any one of the lads out for a dance. On this particular night my friend Liam Burke was asked out to dance. The dance was a fast set, but when I saw Liam on the floor I changed the fast records for slow numbers. I know Liam was not keen on this girl, so he was furious when the tempo changed from fast to slow. He put his fist up at me as he danced slowly by the stage. I thought this was very funny but, needless to say, Liam had the last laugh when later he did the same to me. At this stage I would like to record our thanks to the late Eileen Tiernan, who looked after the ladies' cloakroom. She was a wonderful woman, always in good form, laughing and joking. To make her job a little more comfortable we put a Kosangas heater into the ladies cloakroom, and Eileen would read her *Woman's Way* magazine. Jimmy Dunne of Sallins road was in charge of the gents' cloakroom. This was a more dangerous occupation – Jimmy had no such luxury as a heater and even in those days of the late sixties one or two lads would have consumed too much drink and they would give Jimmy a hard time. Jimmy had a great personality and was always able to talk these lads round, and thankfully he was never assaulted. If there are cloakrooms in heaven it's a fair bet that Eileen and Jimmy are in charge.

The first Old Folks' Party in Clane hall. On the left: Mrs Christina Byrne, Dillie Purcell, Chrissie Gorman, Mrs Farrell, Eileen Tiernan. On the right: Mr Doran, Kathleen Dunne, Jack Farrell, John Walsh.

The Clane Beatles, 1967. Back row: Philly McCormack, Robbie Booth, Paddy Behan, Frank Behan, Fergal Noonan, Peter Burke. Front row: Jim Mahony, Liam Burke, Fr Tom O'Malley, Pat Burke, Joe Bracken, Peter Duffy.

The record hops were a success. We made a profit of £83 over the summer, and we decided to hold an Old Folks' Christmas party in the hall, Clane. A lot of work was done to put decorations up in the hall but we had plenty of help from our friends, Jim and Thomas Mahony, Pat and Peter Burke and Frank, and Simon Behan. The party was a great success and about eighty senior citizens from Clane and the surrounding area really enjoyed themselves. Again, my father's Morris Minor came in very handy for bringing people to and from the party. I remember in particular carrying Peter (Cider), Rourke (Capdoo), and Paddy Stephens (Ballinagappagh). Paddy lived up a short lane and it was very wet and mucky. As I was turning the car on the lane the back wheels were spinning in the mud. Paddy got a bit anxious and said 'will you hurry up, its not the f—kin' Queen Mary you're driving'. The ICA later took over the running of the Senior Citizen's Christmas Parties and have done a brilliant job since our first party.

Father Tom O'Malley was instrumental in forming the Youth Club in Staplestown. A room beside the church was transformed with the aid of large coloured photos of groups such as the Beatles, Davy Jones and the Monkees, the Kinks, and many more on the walls. Coloured lights were also used and gave the room a wonderful atmosphere. Helping Father O'Malley at that time (1967) in Staplestown were Cáit Murphy, Carmel Casey, Tommy Moore, Michael Casey, Morna Hosey, Michael Cosgrove, Ann Casey, Eileen Kelly, Lilly Tuite, Joe Dunne, Sarah Cosgrove, Pat Kelly, Helen Brien, Mary Brien, Paud Brien, Bernie Maher, Tony Brien, Terry Doherty, John Crowe, Tommy Heffernan, Paraic Casey and a wonderful lad, the late Jerome Casey. Bryan, Liam, Jim Mahony, Pat Harty, Joe Duffy and myself enjoyed many great nights at the hops in Staplestown. We were always regarded as friends and to this day we have a great respect for all those mentioned. They in turn supported the hops in Clane hall and came nearly every week. The girls and lads from Smithstown, Johninstown, Rathcoffey and Prosperous also gave us great support – from Smithstown came Kathleen McCartan and Josephine Heneghan, along with Bernadette Giblin from Johninstown. When these three girls met up with Cáit, Carmel and Eileen from Staplestown they really made the hops in Clane. Others I remember well were Margaret McCartan, Mary Byrne, Ann Mitchell, Elizabeth Noonan, Frank Campbell, Tom Campbell, Peter Curran, Evelyn Curran, Bernard Cummins, and Seán Travers – all from the Smithstown/Johninstown area. From Rathcoffey came Tony Doherty, Leo Reilly, Pat Keenan, Paddy Lynch, Seamus Kennedy, Martin Keenan, Frank Keenan, Mary Doran and Joe Doran. From Prosperous we had our old friends Ger and Andy Gannon and John Healy. From Sallins came Lily McCormack, Miriam McCormack, Bridgie Cully, Margaret Walsh, Margaret Cully, Marion Dalton and her late sister Phyllis, who was a great supporter of our hops. She was a beautiful girl and always had that lovely smile. I think Phyllis met her husband, Bernard Cummins, at the hop in Clane.

As well as the hops, we organised Youth Club outings to Tramore, Salthill, Arklow, and Bundoran in the summer. My uncle Edmond supplied the buses and we would stop off for a dance on the way home. I think it was in 1967 that, on the way home from an outing, the buses stopped in Parnell Square, Dublin. My father was driving one of the buses. He parked and made a bed for himself on the back seat while we went dancing. My cousin from Toronto, Michael Flahive, was with us. He was sixteen years old but stood about six feet tall. When we walked up to the door of the National Ballroom, the bouncers would not admit him as he

Members of the Irish Countrywomen's Association.

The Staplestown Roses: Carmel Casey, Cait Murphy, Ann Casey, Eileen Kelly and Morna Hosey in Boyle, County Roscommon, 1967.

Staplestown hall, the old Youth Club.

was not wearing a tie. We went back to the bus and my father took off his tie and gave it to Michael. We went up to the door of the National again only for the bouncers to say, 'sorry, you can't come in, you're wearing denims'. We went back to the bus again and my father said, 'here, try my trousers'. My father's waist was about thirty-eight inches, and Michael's was twenty-eight inches. He tried on my father's trousers and I can still hear him say 'Gee Uncle Pat I don't think this is gonna work'. He stood there and looked a bit like a circus clown with these very wide trousers. We walked around O'Connell Street that night, window-shopping, but we had a good laugh about it after. It was on the 1968 Youth Club Outing to Bundoran that I 'got off' with a young girl, Breeda McIntyre, and we eventually married in 1974.

We held a Parents' Night in Clane hall in 1967. It was a very enjoyable night with plenty of food and drink and music supplied by the late and great Christy Bolger of Sallins. We also held a barbecue that same year. It was held in Manzor's Quarry: at the top end of the football field where Loughbollard Estate is now built. Over 160 people turned up on the night and I think we ran out of burgers. Staplestown Youth Club also ran a Parents' Night that year. It was held in the room above the hop room. A lot of work was put in by the girls and lads and the room was beautiful on the night. The parents really enjoyed it and I believe it is something that could be held today – so all you young people out there get together and organise a Parents' Night in your area.

In 1987 the twenty-first anniversary of the Clane and Staplestown Youth Clubs was celebrated at a function held in Dowlings of Prosperous. A huge crowd turned up and guest of honour was our great friend Rev. Father Tom O'Malley. Supper was served and we danced to the sounds of the sixties. Father O'Malley made a presentation of the proceeds to Matt Browne of the Irish Wheelchair Association.

The Odlums office girls, 1966. Margaret Bryan, Kill, and Lily Tuite, the Range, Donadea.

A very important part of our entertainment in the fifties and sixties was provided by the Ideal Cinema, Prosperous. The cinema was situated where the shopping centre is now. It was owned and run by Paddy (Pop) Price and his sons Ernie and Paddy. Approximately twelve of us from Clane would cycle every Sunday to Price's. They were very enjoyable days – it only cost 6d to get in, which in today's money would be 2 cent. They screened all the big films, and I remember two in particular: *King Kong* and *The Bridge on the River Kwai*. Audie Murphy was our favourite cowboy hero, and we laughed ourselves sick when Old Mother Reilly came on screen. Also, of course, the *Three Stooges* were very popular. Naas cinema at that time was called The Coliseum. We cycled in there a few times – but Prosperous was the number one.

Carnivals of Dancing were held in most places. We went dancing in the marquees in Naas, Robertstown, Coill Dubh, Edenderry, Rathangan, Ballagh Cross, Cloncurry, Kilcock, Maynooth and Leixlip. Many of the top showbands would pack in 2,000 people in these huge canvas tents.

One incident I will never forget happened in Clane marquee in 1970. Loughbollard Estate was being built at that time and many of the block layers and brickies came from Derry. They, like any group, were mostly very nice lads, but a few decided one night during a dance to give trouble. They were quickly ejected by Pa Connolly and the late, great Seán Conneff. They did not go away but went around to the back of the marquee and began to cut the stay ropes. Luckily, someone saw them as they hacked rope after rope and told the committee members. Pa and Seán went around and gave them a few thumps and managed to stop them just before they cut the main stay ropes. Garda Gleeson opened up the barracks and they were glad to run in there to escape from the Clane lads. We went to a dance in a marquee in Leixlip one night in 1968. Imagine our surprise when after paying in we saw about five security men with Alsatian dogs on leashes. Needless to say there was no trouble in that marquee on that night.

Where did they get those socks from? A pioneer outing to Kilkee on 1 July 1971: Patti Cooke, Liam Burke, Breeda McIntyre, and Paddy Behan.

Group presentation to Father T. O'Malley CC.

CLANE & STAPLESTOWN YOUTH CLUBS

Joint

21st Anniversary Celebration

in

DOWLINGS, PROSPEROUS.

on

WEDNESDAY 28th OCTOBER, 1987

9.00p.m. - 1.30a.m.

DISCO - Sounds of the 60's

Subscription (Including Supper) £4.00

Matt Brown and Father T. O'Malley CC.

Joe Byrne, Peter McIntyre, Ann Byrne, Oliver Delaney. Keadeen Hotel, Newbridge 1974.

Sadly the showbands began to lose out to cabaret in the mid-seventies. Patrons now wanted a drink and a bit of comfort when they went out socialising. There were over 800 showbands in Ireland in the sixties and most of them were kept very busy and made a good living. Following on from the cabaret, discos became more popular and the young people preferred disco music. I was sorry to see the decline of the showbands as they were our life in the sixties, but all good things must come to an end, and I am just glad that I was around during that great era.

THE DANDIES

It all started at a hop in Staplestown hall. The Youth Club organised a Parents' Night and Father Tom O'Malley asked Christy and Vincent Brereton and Ritchie Hayden to provide some music during the function, which proved to be a huge success. As the group became more popular, they decided that they needed a drummer. Father O'Malley travelled up to Dublin and bought a second-hand drum kit with the name The New Dandies pasted on the bass drum. They decided then to call themselves The Dandies and John Brereton joined as the drummer. This began the musical journey of The Dandies which continued for a further fifteen years. Pierre Doyle, then owner of Dag Weld's Pub, approached Christy Brereton to play some music and the ballad scene began, with The Dandies performing in 'select lounges' throughout Kildare. John Donoghue was the lead singer and as the years went on, other

The Dandies.

members of the Brereton family joined the group, eventually all eight members of the family were on stage with their black and red uniforms, which Christy's wife Nancy took care of. Other members of The Dandies included Peter and Joss Gordan and Gerry Domican. They also played at a barbecue in Manzor's quarry, now Loughbollard Estate, organised by the Clane Youth Club in the late sixties, with power coming from the battery in Christy's van. Mick Kelleher met his future wife, Marjorie Bracken, at the same function. They were wonderful, happy years, and friendships made then continue to this present day.

VIII

CONKERS, MARBLES, GOING TO THE DOGS AND BALDONNEL

Paddy Behan

The first game we played as children would have been marbles. There were different types of marble games:

Rings: where players put, say, four marbles each into a ring and took it in turns to throw a marble at the ring, hoping to knock a few out of the ring.

Holes: we would make three holes in an even and smooth patch of ground. Each hole would be two inches in diameter. The players would throw their marble at each hole in turn, and the player who successfully got his marble into the three holes first was the winner.

Spanners: for this game a player with a wide span (a big hand) generally won out. The first player threw his marble on the ground, the second player tried to get his marble as close as possible to his opponent's marble, close enough so that he could touch the two marbles with his fingers outstretched.

Certain players were very good at rings – others preferred holes and some liked spanners. Liam Burke loved spanners as he had a very slim hand and long fingers so he had a wide span. Philly McCormack loved rings because when all the marbles were in the ring he would produce a large steel ball-bearing from a lorry or tractor and throw it at the mass of marbles in the ring. If he connected he would knock six or eight marbles from the ring. Eventually we objected to the use of this ball-bearing as we were losing all the time – and anyway, nobody wanted to play rings with Philly, so he reverted to playing with the normal size marble.

The next game we played was conkers. We would go up to Clongowes Wood College and collect chestnuts that had fallen from the trees. Some of us were not satisfied with the windfalls and we used large lumps of wood to knock down even more chestnuts. We were very lucky nobody was badly injured as there would be ten or more of us, all throwing our large pieces of wood up into the trees. We took the chestnuts home, hammered a hole through them and put a piece of string, usually an old shoelace, through the hole and played conkers. Some of the lads would have a small conker but it would be very hard. When one would ask them 'what's your conker?', they would reply 'conker twenty', which meant that they had won twenty games so if you beat his conker twenty with your virgin conker you would be the proud possessor of a conker twenty-one, and all the lads would be dying to have a go at beating you. I remember Liam Burke's elder brother, Vincent, put one of his chestnuts up the chimney for a few weeks to harden. When he took it down it was as hard as the hob of hell. Many lads challenged him, hoping to break his conker, but none ever succeeded. I think from memory, Vincent's conker must have been about conker one hundred.

Another game we loved was pea-shooting. The shooter was about four inches long, and we got that from a weed growing in the ditches. The peas were in fact the seeds of the elder tree or elderberries. We had many hours of fun playing this game and it cost us nothing.

We then turned our hands to old bicycle wheels. We would run behind the wheel, hitting it with a stick as we ran. It was great sport. I remember one day my friend, Thomas Mahony, appeared out with his wheel – this was a luxury model because Thomas had put a tube and tyre onto it. We were all very envious and immediately we went up to Nancy's Lane, hoping to find a tyre for our wheels. In the fifties, Nancy's Lane and Capdoo Lane were used as a dumping ground for certain things – not that there was much dumped because, like in Cuba now, people found a use for nearly everything.

Football was the one game we all loved in the fifties and sixties. I remember around 1957, Rev. Father Hughes CC was driving the school team to Timahoe for a match. He had a Volkswagen car at the time and tried to fit us all in together. Two of us were in the small space between the back seat and the rear window. There were eight or nine packed into the back seat, sitting on top of one another. He put four or five into the front and even after all that two lads were still standing outside the car. Father Hughes then pulled up the bonnet of the Volkswagen, which of course had a rear engine, and he put the two lads, I think it was John Langan and Pat Griffin, under the bonnet. He tied a piece of rope onto the bonnet and one of the lads held the rope in order to keep the bonnet down. Father Hughes was afraid of an accident, so he drove to Clongowes Wood College and a teacher there took half of us in his car to the match in Timahoe. On the way to the match Father Hughes asked, 'Who is going to mark Tommy Byrne?'

Tommy, who lives near Firmount Cross, was a lovely footballer. Gene Smyth's reply to Father Hughes was 'I think you had better put two lads on him Father'.

I also remember playing for the Parish team in Broadford in 1958. It was a cold clear evening. Standing behind the goal I could see two young children, three to four years old. They were in their bare feet, and their father was shouting a lot for Broadford and was very drunk. I thought at the time that a few pairs of shoes would have been a better investment for his children than the many pints he had consumed.

My earliest recollection of being really excited about sport was in 1956 when Kildare won the Leinster. Des Marron was in goal and we all hoped he would go on to win an All-Ireland medal, but it was not to be. Galway had a great team around that time and many of us took on the names of famous footballers. I remember Billy Barrett of Richardstown called himself Jack Mahon after the Galway goalkeeper. My brother, Frank, called himself Frankie Stockwell and Mick Cooney called himself after Seán Purcell, two great Galway forwards.

I remember listening to the mile in the Olympic games of 1956 in Melbourne. I can still hear the commentator shouting, 'Delaney's kicking, Delaney's kicking' as Ronnie came from behind, like a good horse, to win the gold medal. Ronnie was only twenty-one when he won the gold and beat two great runners, Brian Hewson of Great Britain and John Landy of Australia. In 1956 it took three days to fly from Ireland to Australia via New York, San Francisco and Hawaii. It was worth the long journey for the Irish athletes, as Fred Teidt of Dublin won a silver medal and Tony Byrne, Johnny Caldwell, and Freddie Gilroy won bronze medals in boxing.

We always enjoyed the camogie matches played in Manzor's field, where Loughbollard Estate is now. Ned Coughlan, a Wexford man, who worked in Paddy Woods' garage, was team manager. Some of these games could turn rough, and I remember in particular my aunts Molly Lavin (Delaney) and Chrissie Lavin (O'Toole). Molly was a great player and used to run the game exhorting her team to play even harder. Most of the opposition were a bit nervous of Molly as she used to go in very hard and never draw back, and besides that she was a very skilful player. Also, I remember players like Patti and Josie Doyle, Anne Fallon, Mary Joe Farrell, Chris Coady, Rose Healy and the Kenny sisters, Maura and Breda (mother of John Finn, Kildare footballer and All-Star). We would hang around the sideline and as soon as a player broke her hurley we dashed out to capture the two pieces of broken hurley which we repaired the following day.

In the later sixties Father Bryan Cullen SJ, Clongowes Wood College, founded a Society known as the SRPA: the Society for the Relief of the Poor and Aged. Father Cullen drew up a list of people from Clane, Prosperous and Rathcoffey, all of whom were elderly and mostly living alone. Some of the Clongowes Wood College students joined the Society and put a lot of work into raising funds for the Society. My uncle, Edmond Behan, of Main Street, Clane, gave Father Cullen the use of one of his mini-buses every Saturday free of charge. I was the driver and with Bryan and Liam, would go up to Clongowes Wood College and collect the students. We would then go to John Blake's shop in Clane where Londis now stands. John Blake was a very decent man also, and gave Father Cullen all the provisions at cost price. We would load up the mini-bus with about forty sliced pans, thirty pounds of butter, twenty pounds of tea, forty pounds of sugar, forty bales of briquettes, 200 cigarettes, and plug tobacco The student in charge of the list would accompany us to each house and give the householder provisions for the week ahead. At each house, two or three students would do some work like painting, cleaning, cutting hedges and/or weeding. Also, they would have a chat with the elderly person over a cup of tea, and I believe more was thought of the chat and company than anything else. Those students all came from wealthy backgrounds and I was amazed and delighted to see how they got down to business and did so much good work, sometimes in pretty awful conditions. They never complained and enjoyed what they did and kept in contact with those old people for years afterwards.

One incident from that time stands out in my memory. We called to a house outside Clane where two old ladies resided. It was a hot May day and the house was a bit run-down. When Bryan, Liam and myself went inside, we were amazed at the number of flies in the kitchen – they were everywhere – landing on the milk bottle, the loaf of bread and the butter, which were all on the table. We asked the old ladies if we could get rid of the flies and one of the ladies replied, 'Musha – sure what harm are they doing?' We drove down to John Blake's shop and purchased two cans of fly killer. We asked the old ladies to step outside for a few minutes while we sprayed the interior. Ten minutes later there were dead flies everywhere – we swept them from the floor and filled a large bag with dead flies. The two old ladies were not impressed as they were so used to the flies – they missed their company.

Around 1957 the Russians launched their satellite, or sputnik, into space. My father would set the alarm for 3.30a.m. and nearly everyone in St Brigid's Terrace would be out staring up into the night sky to see a small white light, like a moving star, make its way across the sky. I suppose we felt a bit like the three wise men, but we did not follow, and as soon as the light disappeared we ran back to bed.

Outside John Blake's shop – Martin Connolly, Bridie Synnott and Patti Doyle.

We're only here for the beer: I.D.T. O'Connell Street, Dublin, 1952. Patsy Farrell, Philip McIntyre, Jim Brien.

Back row: John Harrington, Trish Connolly, Marie Walshe, Seán O'Hara, Teresa Hayes, and Pat Lynam. Front row: Pat Burke and Mary Monaghan. Comedy Act in Clane GAA Hall. Early eighties.

In 1960 the UN asked Ireland to send troops to the Congo. When we heard that the soldiers were flying out from Baldonnel, Liam Burke, my brother Simon and myself decided we would cycle there. We did not know where Baldonnel was but when we got to Celbridge we asked a man for directions. 'Go out the Hatch road', he told us, so we continued on. After about three miles, this huge aeroplane flew low over us – it was an American transport plane – a Globemaster. We thought we were at the airport then but we still had a good few miles to go. When we eventually reached Baldonnel the plane had landed. It was massive and two columns of troops were boarding on two ramps. I suppose about 300 men marched onto the plane and then they drove land rovers and armoured cars onto the plane. They drove so many onto the plane you would think they were coming out the other side. When it was full and they started the engines the wind from the engines would knock you down – dried grass from the recently cut lawns flew everywhere. It made one feel small when such a huge aeroplane taxied out onto the runway and eventually took off. Everyone cheered and we felt so proud of our young Irish peacemakers flying out to a very dangerous situation in what was then the Belgian Congo. Little did anyone realize that some of these fine brave men would never see Ireland again.

On 10 November 1960 a UN patrol of Irish troops was ambushed by Baluba tribesmen in northern Katanga. Eleven members of A Company, 33rd Battalion, put up a brave fight against hundreds of Baluba tribesmen near Niemba, but were overwhelmed, and ten men lost their lives. The ten dead were Lieutenant Kevin Gleeson, Sergeant Hugh Gaynor, Corporal Peter Kelly, Corporal William Dougan, Trooper Anthony Browne, Private Matthew Farrell, Private Thomas Fennell, Trooper Thomas Kelly, Private Gerard Killeen and Private Michael McGuinn. One man, Private Joseph Fitzpatrick, though badly injured, survived. Private Fitzpatrick afterwards stated that he owed his life to Trooper Anthony Browne. We will never forget the sacrifice those men made in the cause of world peace.

HEROES OF NIEMBA

In a lonely Congo jungle
Some six thousand miles away
Ten brave soldiers of old Ireland
Were engaged in deathly fray
With Balubas fierce and savage
Who attacked so mercilessly
And our gallant green-clad troopers
Were outnumbered hopelessly.

Lieutenant Gleeson walking towards them
With raised arm said 'Jambo'
But that arm soon was shattered
With an arrow from a bow
Sons of Erin, he commanded
Level guns and open fire

May your aim be true and steady
And God's mercy your desire.

Pat Behan
(1919-1973)

Carol Singing, Dogs and More Work and Play

Talking of peace brings me to Christmas and carol singing. Clane carol singers used to perform in hotels and pubs around the county and even into Dublin. I remember in 1958 the carol singers met outside Manzor's in Clane. There were about ten car-loads of us. I jumped into the car of Mr Costello, the principal of the boy's National School. We went first to Osberstown House Hotel, Sallins, now the private residence of Renault's Bill Cullen. We then proceeded to the Grand Hotel in Newbridge, then to the Dew Drop Inn, Kill, and from there into Dublin City. I remember I could see the road through a hole in the floor of Mr Costello's old Ford Prefect car. After singing in some hotel in Dublin and as we drove through the city, a garda squad car flashed us down. Mr Costello stopped his car and the garda informed him

The Clane carol singers, 1962. Back row: Vincent Burke, Michael Bracken, Joe McCormack, Moira Burke, Berna McManmon, Phil McCormack, Seán Cullen, Gene Smith, Philip O'Neill, Esther McCormack, Mary McManmon, Breda Behan, Ann Corrigan, Vera Higgins, Maura Corrigan, Billy Curran, Liam Higgins, Seán McManmon, Peggy McCormack, Jim Mahony. Front row: Brendan Langan, Frankie Behan, Pat Burke, Phil McCormack, Liam Burke.

that he was driving without lights. Mr Costello apologised and told the garda that we were carol singers out collecting money for charity and the garda said 'Ok, go ahead, but make sure your lights are on'.

My uncle, Edmond Behan, had buses and hire-cars. Ned and Bill Ennis used to hire Edmond's mini-buses to drive them to the dogs. The Ennis brothers were known all over Ireland for training greyhounds. They called their dogs Clane Salmon, Clane Trout, Clane Pike, and so on. I used to drive the mini-buses and went to the dogs in Navan, Mullingar, Shelbourne Park, Harold's Cross, and Edenderry. The mini-buses were Volkswagens with the engine in the back.

One cold night we were heading to Mullingar when Ned asked me to let down my window a bit to give the dogs some air. I let the window down an inch or so as it was a cold windy night. After a few miles Ned asked me to let it down even further. What Ned didn't realise was that the dogs were lying over the engine and the heat from it had nearly put the dogs to sleep. If I had told Ned about the engine heat he would have put the dogs into the front, sitting on my knee as I drove.

Ned and Bill were lovely men and great craic. Ned told me that he had nearly died during the Great Flu of 1918. Millions died in Europe from the Spanish Flu, and Ned was lucky to survive. He was about fifteen years old at the time and he said he drank buckets of well water and eventually got better. Ned and Bill introduced me to all the great greyhound trainers of the 1960s. Ned hated if his dog had drawn box number four – he called number four the 'coffin box'. We still miss Ned and Bill – they were two of nature's gentlemen.

Another man I liked very much was Tom McEvoy, the father of Tony McEvoy CC Tom was a retired Detective Garda and used to take the field at the top of St Brigid's Terrace, to sow potatoes. He asked me to help him drop the potatoes. I was about eight years old at the time and I'm nearly sure I dropped the potatoes into the drills, leaving a very small space between each potato. There would normally be about twelve inches between each spud and I would guess that Tom had probably to go over all I had done and rearrange the potatoes. But he never complained and I was pleasantly surprised when he gave me a lovely red 10s note. It was the first money I had ever earned and to put it into perspective, two years later we were paid 8s for picking potatoes in Clongowes Wood College – working from 8.00a.m. to 6.00p.m., so you can see from this what a generous man Tom McEvoy was.

Another man who was very good to us was Tommy Doyle (Main Street, Clane), Patti McCormack's father. Tommy had a few fields around Clane and used to hire us to work for him. He was a very fair man and when he generously paid us he also asked if we were happy with what we got. He might not have bothered to ask – all he had to do was look at our happy faces.

We worked picking potatoes in Clongowes Wood College and we also picked fruit in the garden there. Jimmy Nestor and his uncle, also Jimmy, were the gardeners. Young Jimmy gave us wooden boxes and into these we put the gooseberries. When full, we emptied the boxes into very large wooden containers in the garden shed. There must have been tons of gooseberries in that shed when we had finished. I'd say gooseberry tart was on the menu in the college for months on end. We also picked strawberries, raspberries, plums, pears and apples. It was a beautiful garden and Brother Adams was in charge at that time.

We graduated from the garden to thinning turnips. The drills were very long as the field itself was about thirty acres. We would thin one and a half drills per day at 15s per drill. It was

Mrs Doyle going to Mass.

hard work but we were glad of it. I remember one summer was very dry and hot. The drills became hard and our fingers were skinned. Jim Mahony, Pat Griffin, the Kerry and Kildare footballer, and myself used to go over very early in the morning when the dew was on the ground. We would work until twelve o'clock and then stop as the sun baked the ground hard. In the evening we would return and work until 10.30p.m. Pat Griffin, even though he was from a farming background, got fed up after three days and went home. Jim Mahony and I kept going until we had the thinning finished about one month later.

Around 1958 my good friend Liam 'Busty' Higgins asked me if I wanted some summer work in Blackhall Stud. I was delighted to get the job as the Stud paid well and Liam and I had a great time working there. Liam's father, Bill, worked there for years and the manager was a Mr Jeffers. Lord Astor, who owned the Stud, came over once a year and Liam and I had to make sure we pulled up any ragwort – buchaláinn, we called them – before Lord Astor arrived. Lord Astor sold the Stud to another English man who died young. Sheik Mohammed then bought the Stud and has spent millions refurbishing it and building new houses and boxes. It is a beautiful place now and in the capable hands of Clane man Michael Murphy, who is manager.

Later we heard of work available at Andy Byrne's farm in Longtown. His foreman, Paddy Connolly, of Firmount, a lovely man and a great cyclist, told his brother Tommy to look out for a few lads. Tommy duly contacted Liam Burke, Fergal Noonan, Willie Dunne, Gerry Dunne and myself and we went to work for Mr Byrne. He was a very decent man and paid us over the odds: £5 per week. We dropped potatoes, thinned turnips, hoed mangolds, stacked bales of hay, and topped, using the tractor and mowing bar. Everyone wanted to drive the tractor and Andy's son, Anthony, willingly let us drive when he could easily have driven himself all day long. Anthony is still a great friend of ours and we meet him in Naas Tennis Club during the various tournaments there.

The men who worked for the local farmers were a great bunch. They worked very hard, hail, rain or snow and knew everything about farming. The first of these men was Pat Quinn. He worked for farmer John McEvoy who lived in a fine house beside the church, now owned by Marie's Antiques. Pat was very kind to me, buying me ice-cream anytime he met me in my grandfather's shop. He was very fond of playing cards and used to visit Kit and Nan McCormack's house, on the Doctor's road and also my grandfather's house where they played cards into the early hours.

Another of these men was John Walsh, father of Pat Walsh of Half-Mile-Bridge, and of Rose Langan. John looked after the farm of Mr Daly, who lived where Manzor's shop in Main Street is today. John would often call in to my grandfather's shop and buy sweets, biscuits and minerals for his son Pat. I remember Pat would always share what he had with me.

Paddy Delaney of Capdoo was a cobbler. He would heel and sole shoes for a very reasonable price. He lived in a lovely little thatched house in Capdoo. I remember he had an old BSA motorbike in one of the rooms and we were fascinated by it. We would call to collect the shoes on a Saturday and sometimes Paddy would not have had time to do the job so he would ask us to come back on Sunday morning around 10.00a.m. He would finish off repairing the shoes while we watched. Then the church bell would ring at 10a.m. for 10.30 Mass and we would get a bit anxious but Paddy was an easy-going man and got the shoes done just in time for Mass.

Picking mushrooms was another great pastime. The best field for this was the brickfield in Clongowes Wood and the best time was about 7.00a.m. That field would be white with mushrooms and some mornings we would have more than we could carry. We threaded the stalk of the mushrooms onto a long wild plant growing in the field. We called these hanks. On the way home sometimes a motorist would stop and we would sell them a hank or two for 1s. Wild mushrooms were ten times nicer than the cultivated type and we would fry them with a rasher and sausage or put them onto a long fork, putting a lump of butter and some salt into the cup of the mushroom and hold them over the open fire. They were delicious.

Another thing we enjoyed was robbing orchards. I remember some of the boys in the National School robbed Marron's Orchard in the Main Street. The headmaster got wind of it and held a 'mini-tribunal', but it all came to nothing and nobody was proved guilty. Tony McEvoy's father, Tom, had a nice orchard beside his house at the hall in Clane. Pat Griffin, the Kildare and Kerry footballer, fancied robbing it. He told me he would keep watch and I could go in and rob the apples and if I did he would give me half of what I robbed – talk about a Kerry joke. Needless to say I could not bring myself to rob Mr McEvoy's orchard because he had been so decent to me years before.

Peter Wallace, P.J.'s father, had a nice orchard behind his house and bicycle shop on Main Street. One evening a group of us had congregated at Manzor's Corner. Peter McManmon had come back home on holiday from England. Peter told a few of the lads to rob Mr Wallace's orchard while he kept watch. Peter gave the lads about five minutes and then went up to Mr Wallace's front door and rang the bell. Mr Wallace answered the door and Peter informed him that a few lads were robbing his orchard. Mr Wallace thanked Peter for being so honest and took a sweeping brush out to his orchard and prodded the lads down from the trees. The lads could not figure out how they had been rumbled, but Peter and myself had a good laugh about it then, and years later when we recalled it.

My grandfather, Paddy Lavin, had a general grocery shop where Spar is now. He did a great trade and had nearly everything in his shop. Most items were loose in those days: biscuits would come in large tins and would be weighed out in quarter, half, or one-pound bags, as requested by the customer. Likewise with sweets like bull's-eyes, acid drops, Yorkshire toffees and Scot's Clan. They were in large glass jars and people generally bought a quarter-pound.

My grandfather used to go to Clongowes Wood College about twice a month and purchase a large bath of dripping. It would take two men to load and unload it. Everyone loved to have their rashers and sausages fried in the college dripping. I remember Emily O'Rourke, who lived with her uncle Garret in a small house across the road from Tony McKenna's shop. She asked me for one pound of dripping, so I cut large pieces of dripping with a bacon knife and put them into a brown bag and slapped it up onto the weighing scales. As I took it off, Emily shouted at me to put it back on the scales, as the indicator hand on the scales had not stopped moving. When I put it back on the scales, the hand stopped at fifteen ounces – one ounce short of a pound. 'Now', she said 'put more dripping into that bag and don't be rushing when you weigh something'. Grandfather also sold pigs' heads and crubeens and I was always amazed at how quickly they sold out – I thought they looked terrible. Most people when they did their shopping did not pay with cash. What they bought would be entered into 'the book'. My granny at the end of each week had to total up all the various pages. She had no adding machine – she did it all in her head and sometimes when she was near the end of a tot someone, usually Grandfather, would interrupt her and she would have to start all over again.

Doctor M.J. Walsh, General Practitioner for the Clane area, was a wonderful doctor. He had time for everyone, rich or poor. He went to Mass every morning and I remember, while serving Mass, occasionally a person would tiptoe into the church and ask Dr Walsh to attend someone who was dying. Dr Walsh lived and had his surgery where the Father John Sullivan Centre is today. He would leave all the tablets, cough bottles and so on out on the mantelpiece of the waiting room for collection. The door was always open so a person just walked in and looked for their name on the round tablet box or cough bottle. How times have changed. Dr Walsh smoked Craven A cigarettes and my granny always made sure she ordered a carton from the supplier. His wife was a beautiful woman – he had a large photo of her hanging over his fireplace. They were only married a year or so when she died. The famous Doctor Andy Rynne then came to Clane as did Doctor Xavier Flanagan. These two men have looked after us so well for the past twenty years or more.

Aunt Mollie Delaney (with baby Paddy), Pat Quinn, Aunt Statia Behan (with baby Ann), and myself, enjoying ice cream given to me by my great friend Pat.

Happy children in St Brigid's terrace, 1958. From left to right: Jackie McCormack, John Delaney, Martin (Murt) Nevin.

Part of a weekly shop bill from Lavin's, Clane.

Sergeant Stokes, Gardaí McGuinness, Jim O'Donnell (Snr), and Paddy Aherne were stationed in Clane Garda Station on the Main Street when we were young. Garda Paddy Aherne loved a game of cards and every weekend he would visit my grandfather Paddy Lavin and along with a few more would play cards until the early hours. Paddy was a very nice man and one day he said to me 'Come on and I will show you the Black Hole' – the detention room in the Garda Station was known locally as the Black Hole. The room was very bare – there was a wooden bed raised about four inches from the floor, with a few blankets. There was a channel in the floor which ran up to a square opening in the bottom of the outside wall – this was the toilet. It frightened me and I remember saying to myself that I will never spend a night in jail. In those days you could be done for very minor offences, like riding bicycles three abreast.

Not having a light on your bicycle was another common offence. I remember cycling up by Paddy Woods' garage one night and the battery in my lamp was practically gone. Garda Jim O'Donnell, father of Seamus (Capdoo), stopped me. He said 'You have no light'. I replied 'Yes I have'. He looked at it and said 'I have to shine my torch on your lamp to see the glimmer'. He did not summons me and let me off, telling me to buy a new battery the next day.

CLANE GARDA STATION

Sergeants:

Peter Marron, Charles Stokes, Richard O'Leary, James Davis, William Egan, Hugh Donnelly, Frank McLoughlin and John Nolan.

Up Wexford! Sergeant Stokes outside the Clane
barracks.

GARDAÍ:

Maurice Lee, Thomas McGuinness, Paddy Ahern, James O'Donnell, Maurice Shortt, James
Nesdale, Owen Doyle, Patrick McCabe, James Kelly, John Daly, William Kiernan, Brendan
O'Brien, John Riney, Pat McLoughlin, William White, Ted Coughlan, Hubert Fagan, Martin
Gleeson, Michael Kelleher, Michael McGann, Noel Cumiskey, Philip Timoney, Francis
Ward, John Robbin, Pat Walsh, Peter Ryan, Michael Browne, Cornelius O'Mahony, Daniel
Stapleton, Philip Farrell and Trevor Maye.

My father drove a bread van for Cunningham's Bakery in Naas in the 1950s. One summer's
evening, he and two other men from Sallins were cycling three abreast when the Naas squad
car came up on them. The garda took out his notebook and asked the first man for his name
and address. He did likewise with the second man. These two men lived in St Brigid's Terrace,
Sallins, and the garda assumed my father's address must be Sallins, but it was St Brigid's Terrace,
Clane. The two lads were fined 2/6d. and my father never received a summons. With six or
seven children at that time I'm sure he was very happy to escape a fine.

During the summer of 1956 myself and my brothers Frank and Simon would get the 8.00a.
m. bus to Naas and walk up to Basin Street where Cunningham's Bakery was situated. When
my father's bread van was loaded we all hopped in and away we went. I remember he delivered
bread to Dr Michael Purcell's house at Cooleragh. Dr and Mrs Purcell had two beautiful
daughters and they would buy about a dozen cream buns while their mother bought bread.
Imagine my shock when I saw before my eyes the girls breaking up the buns and throwing
them to the chickens and hens. In those days we would follow a crow for a bun and I was
very close to following those hens. Later in the day Daddy would stop beside the lake at
Poulaphouca and we would have a lovely lunch of fresh cakes and buns washed down with
bottles of Sláinte orange – this was real happiness.

WON PRIZES IN CLANE CONTEST
(1964)

The Gardens Competition in1964, featuring Pat Behan, Mrs McManmon and Jim Lecky.

Joe 'France' Bracken.

Sisters Ann Lecky and Katie Geoghegan, photographed at the rear of Tommy Doyle's house on Main street.

Patsy Gorman lived in a small cottage on the Sallins side of the Liffey Bridge, which was demolished about five years ago. Patsy lived there with his sister Chrissie and Joe 'France' Bracken. France was a great man for the football and like Seán Cribbin and Joe 'Magee' Bracken, kept the game alive and well in Clane. France looked after the school teams and never missed a match. He would give great advice to the young players and never lost his temper no matter what went wrong. We will never forget him.

Patsy Gorman spent some years in Hazel Hall Nursing home following the death of his beloved sister Chrissie. He was very happy in Hazel Hall and would come out every Thursday

Josie Doyle, Chrissie Lavin, Betty
Casey.

to visit Jones' pub where he enjoyed a few pints. He told me one day that he remembered the
Black and Tans, who were stationed in Naas Barracks, where the Court Hotel is today, coming
into Clane. They were very dangerous men and a law unto themselves. Patsy saw them stealing
bottles of stout and whiskey from Geoghegan's pub. They put the bottles up on the high wall
of the Abbey and took out their pistols and took pot shots shattering the bottles. They also shot
hens belonging to Mrs Timmons, who lived opposite the Royal Oak pub. Paddy O'Haran,
owner of the Royal Oak, told me that the Black and Tans always paid for their drinks, because
of the name of the pub. They wrongly assumed that Paddy's grandfather was a royalist.

To get back to Patsy Gorman, he was a great man for poaching salmon from the Liffey. Patsy told
me that he met Sergeant Marron in Clane one day and the Sergeant said to him: 'I know Gorman
you are poaching and one of these nights I will catch you'. Of course Patsy denied he was ever a
poacher. A few nights later Patsy was poaching beside the Liffey Bridge and succeeded in landing
a twelve-pound salmon. Just then he heard Sergeant Marron and Garda Lee up above him on the
bridge. He heard Sergeant Marron remark to Garda Lee 'We will catch Gorman tonight – I can
feel it in my bones'. Patsy lay on top of the fish at the side of the river, trying to hide in the rushes
and trying to keep the fish from thrashing about. He could see two torches flashing their beams of
light down towards him – they appeared to him like searchlights, but in reality were quite weak and
Patsy was not discovered. He told me that that fish was the nicest one he had ever eaten.

Going to Dublin in the 1950s was a very rare event. I remember around 1955 my aunt Rita
(Fanning) and my aunt Martha took me to a pantomime in Dublin – I think it was in the Olympia
and the pantomime was *Dick Whittington and his Cat*. It was absolutely brilliant and to this day I can
remember the beautiful stage sets – one in particular had the most amazing waterfall in it.

Another outing to Dublin was around 1958. My aunt Chrissie (O'Toole) took me to
the Railway Cup Football Final in Croke Park. Josie and Patti Doyle came along too and I
remember we had lunch in an upstairs restaurant in O'Connell Street called The Maple Leaf.
It was a lovely place and for me it was my first time in a restaurant – I have been in many
since but none could compare to that first one –The Maple Leaf.

Fashion 1972.

FASHION AND HAIR

In the 1950s there was no barber shop in Clane, so when one needed a haircut it meant catching the 6.20p.m. bus to Naas and calling into Callaghan Brothers barber shop on Main Street, or George Guilfoyle, Basin Street, Naas. It cost 6d for the bus fare and 1s for the haircut. Jim Malone opened the first barber shop in Clane in the 1960s and it was a great success. Jim was a brilliant barber and a great man with the old cutthroat razor. Many's the time we sat and watched as he went surgeon-like about his task, but never once did he cause blood to flow.

Mai Fielding had a small drapery shop where Classy Lass is today. She stocked mostly ladies' and children's wear and many people had to travel to Kerrigans or Menswear in Naas for their suit and shoes. Some people would get the 8.30a.m. bus to Dublin and would shop in Clery's and Roches Stores. They would return to Clane on the 6.00p.m. bus. If we saw them arrive with bags bearing the name Arnott's we used to say 'those people must be well off to shop there' – I suppose the young people now say something similar when they see bags with the Brown Thomas name.

We did not have much style in the sixties, just a few jackets and pants and one pair of 'good shoes'. I remember looking at the Beatle boots and longing to have a pair but they were too expensive. Penneys opened their first store in Ireland in Mary Street, Dublin, around 1968. They stocked some lovely style at very reasonable prices and we always bought something there when we went to Dublin. I remember going to Dublin one day around 1969 with my cousin Edmond Behan. We both needed a haircut and we called into a place in O'Connell Street called Scissors. It was a large salon situated in a basement room. There were about fifteen stylists, both male and female. We were a bit reluctant to sit in the chair, when this lovely girl of about nineteen called our names. It was the first time ever we had our hair cut by a girl, but it was not the last.

IX

PEOPLE MAKE A DIFFERENCE

Fergal Lee

By all accounts, Clane was a fairly vibrant place towards the end of the nineteenth century. We read stories of great sports meetings, with brass bands parading on the Main Street, the building of a magnificent new church, the arrival of the Presentation Sisters and the foundation of the GAA. Exciting times indeed.

However, from what I can recall of it, the village in the 1940s had declined considerably and was pretty desolate. I was born and reared in the centre of the village, in a house more recently known as The Rowantree, now Given's Opticians. Out of approximately thirty houses on the Main Street, only four had young children. The remainder were occupied by elderly bachelors and spinsters. I could name about thirty of them. Indeed they were all lovely people and I have nothing but fond memories of them, but the composition of the community did not lend itself to vibrancy.

What would today's mobile addicts think of a village with no public phone, with just one party line serving the post office, the Garda Station and the doctor's residence, with all calls monitored by the postmistress? There was no cinema either, or disco or chipper, and alcohol was a definite non-runner for teenagers.

One of the first signs of change was the arrival of two young curates in the early fifties: Father Willie Hughes and Father John O'Leary. They replaced Father Gleeson and Father Mooney – two decent men, but very much in the traditional mode. When passing the curate's house on the Prosperous road a few days later, I saw something that convinced me that change was inevitable. There were the two new priests, stripped to the waist and armed with axes and a crosscut saw. They were clearing the overgrown trees from around the house to allow the sunlight in, and they were chopping up the firewood to supplement their meagre fuel allowance. It was the first time I ever saw a priest without the black serge and Roman collar, and engaged in manual labour.

Within a short period, Father O'Leary had persuaded the parish priest to invest in a film projector and he established a cinema night every Thursday in the village hall. It was run as a fundraiser for the parish, but more importantly it was a major social outlet for the youth. It was our introduction to Hollywood, and the never-ending saga of Batman and Robin. Not to be outdone, Father Hughes established a boxing club in the hall, and bit by bit the sleepy village awoke from its slumber.

Another person who impacted on village life at that time was Louis Dalton. Natives of Tipperary, the Daltons came to Clane around 1950. They lived in the big house now occupied by Dr Flanagan. Louis was a flamboyant character and a great organiser. He was one of the

Mrs McManmon and Alice Donagher
– how does your garden grow?

Pat Donagher on Main Street, Clane, during rush-hour

main movers organising the An Tostal celebrations in Clane in 1954. This was a government-sponsored national festival, presumably designed to lift the spirits of the nation. In Dublin the event was marked by the placing of a Bowl of Light on O'Connell Bridge. True to form, this was dumped into the Liffey a few nights later. In Clane the event was marked by the planting of trees along the Main Street (I think there is still one survivor). The street was also festooned with bunting and the An Tostal flags – maroon with a gold harp. The committee also organised dances in a marquee on the Prosperous road where Liffey Lawns now is. For the first time in Clane we had the big band sounds of Victor Sylvester, Norman Metcalf and Mick Delahunty.

Louis Dalton also organised a children's party in the hall at Christmas. I still remember Santa (Kevin O'Neill) with his Alsatian dog in a harness, pulling a small cart loaded with toys up the hill past Woods' garage to the hall. To fund this event a large carol-singing group was organised. Here again there were no half measures. All the males were togged out with top hats, black cloaks and white cravats, while the ladies wore red cloaks with hoods. Transport was organised to bring the group on a tour of the major pubs in Dublin where lots of money was collected.

Another personality firmly embedded in my memories of that period is the famous Ned Cash. In the forties, Ned and his family lived in a house, since demolished, on the south bank of the Liffey beside the weir. From there they moved, in the fifties, to a new home – a ranch-style timber house, surrounded by a timber stockade, situated at the bottom of the village green where Campbell Tyres now operate.

Childminders Cora Mahony, Martha Behan and Mary Booth with David Mahony, Colm Behan and baby Betty McCormack on the Prosperous road, 1962.

Ned was a larger-than-life character. He was tough, fit, an outstanding horseman and a great judge of horses. He established a stable yard on the site of the old Forge beside the bridge on the Millicent road. Ned had a family of six sons and one daughter, a very welcome addition to a village starved of youth.

The stable was a great attraction for young boys in the village and the affable Ned made all welcome. There we experienced all aspects of the trade: breaking, long-reining, lunging, and show jumping, we watched the farrier (Phil Purcell), saw tooth extractions, tail docking, blistering – we saw it all. When we gained a little experience we were allowed to ride out horses at exercise, which was a special treat. However, it had its moments. I recall a spirited horse bolting one day with Paddy McManmon on board. He went just as we were leaving the yard. Paddy was a hardy fellow but his best efforts failed to control the animal. He stormed around the bend at the Corner House and galloped at full tilt out the Prosperous road with sparks flying from his shoes. Luckily, Jim Cash, mounted on an even livelier horse, was on the scene, and he took off in pursuit. They were almost at Firmount Hill before Jim got up alongside, grabbed the bridle and brought them to a halt. Could you imaging that happening in today's traffic? The bold Paddy, though frightened, had hung on for dear life and was delighted to get his feet back on the ground. I think he went missing from the riding pool for a few weeks after that.

I recall a particular unbroken horse, who, when exercised, could pop over almost any fence with ease on a lunge, but did not take kindly to the saddle. Ned was expecting a likely buyer of such a horse the next day, but knew that this party would not be interested in an unbroken horse. Cometh the hour, cometh the man. Ned brought the horse into the enclosed yard, where he was saddled up with great difficulty. He then called on Jim and Chaw, both of whom were expert horsemen, and he challenged them to mount the smouldering animal. They both declined. Shaking his head in disgust, Ned vaulted into the saddle himself, while the rest of us ran for cover. Peering out from the safety of the harness room door, we witnessed the greatest live rodeo show of all time, as the raging horse reared and bucked and contorted at every possible angle in a bid to unseat Ned, but the main man was not for moving. The show continued for about fifteen minutes before the horse finally relented and submitted to Ned's control.

'Open the gate' he barked and he then rode the horse at full gallop out the Millicent road. He returned to the green minutes later where he popped him over a few poles. The job was complete, and a smiling Ned rode victoriously back into the yard, while Jim and Chaw looked on shamefacedly. The expected buyer arrived next day and the sale was made.

Ned Cash opened the way to many new adventures for us in the fifties. We made trips, in horseboxes, to point-to-point meetings around the country, where our finances were often improved through the benefit of inside information, and of course, there was also the annual pilgrimage to Punchestown. I remember a special day circa 1953, when Jim Cash, aged fourteen, won the Bishopscourt Cup on his father's horse You Mind Me. I believe he was the youngest jockey ever to do so.

Is that a Pioneer pin? Seán Delaney and George Harrington.

Kitty McIntyre and Dolly Stack on O'Connell Street in Dublin, 1953: 'We're going home to Clane, our feet are killing us.'

Off on their honeymoon – Jack and Cathy Kelly, with Mick Giblin in the background.

Another unforgettable outing was a trip to Chipperfield's Circus in the grounds of St Bricin's Hospital, Infirmary Road, Dublin. Flagged as 'the Greatest Show on Earth', this event would definitely be out of our reach at the time, both in terms of distance and cost. However, Ned was acquainted with the Chipperfield family, having sold horses to them over the years, and the ringmaster issued an invitation to Ned and his family for the Saturday show. Somehow the word spread around the village, and as Ned prepared to travel on Saturday morning, he noticed that his family had grown from seven to about twenty-seven. Without saying a word, Ned simply abandoned the car and loaded us all into the horsebox. At the entrance to the big top, Ned ushered us all inside with a pat on the back, saying 'that's another one of mine', while Chipperfield looked on with a knowing grin. All of Clane got ringside seats to the greatest show on earth.

Speaking of the greatest show on earth reminds me of Price's Picture House in Prosperous. I am not referring to the more recent edifice known as the Ideal Ballroom, but the original timber and canvas structure with its mud floor and bench seats. The late Mr Price has to be one of my heroes of the fifties, for providing a run of films as good as, if not better than, those of most big venues in the country. My particular memory is of the film *Rock around the Clock*, which was in Prosperous within days of being screened in Dublin. The riotous behaviour of the Dublin fans was not repeated in Prosperous, but the impact of the new music was the same. The dancing on Price's mud floor generated a cloud of dust that almost obliterated the screen.

X

BRIDIE CONNOLLY NÉE SYNNOTT

Margaret McEvoy

Many of Clane's native residents had the privilege of knowing Bridie Connolly, a most wonderful character who, as one new resident named her, was 'the Mother Teresa of Clane'.

Bridie was born in 1923 in Oulart, Gorey, County Wexford. Orphaned at an early age, she spent much of her childhood in an orphanage. Then, in the late 1940s or early 1950s, she came to Clane to work in John Blake's shop, VG, on the Main Street. In 1966 Bridie married Martin Connolly, a tailor in Clongowes Wood College. The marriage took place in Clane parish church. The couple lived happily in their family home in The Cott. They adopted two lovely daughters, Mary and Olive. In 1992 Martin died, and Bridie was broken-hearted. Her daughters were soon married and living in their own homes, so Bridie was back where she started again.

If anyone seemed to be in need in any way, Bridie very discreetly saw to that need, always treating the person with the utmost dignity. She had an incredible sense of humour, was a brilliant card player and a very loyal friend. In these days when life is very easy for many, it is hard to imagine that each month Bridie delivered in excess of 300 copies of *The Sacred Heart Messenger*. Some were given to people who were at Mass, others went to people whom Bridie would see on the street or the road. Immediately she would abandon her red Ford Fiesta and hand over the magazine with a friendly word.

Until the day she died on 12 January 1999, Bridie was a light to all who knew her. Her sense of humour, her unbelievable faith, her kindness to all those who crossed her path, made her someone never to be forgotten, and indeed we never will forget this diminutive woman who so richly deserved the title of 'Mother Teresa of Clane'.

Ladies' day out: Chrissie Lavin, Bridie Synnott, Chrissie Brilly, Patti Doyle.

The happy bride… Jack Cribbin, Bridie Connolly, Mrs Cribbin.

Clane Parish Church.

XI

ABBEYLANDS

Charlie O'Neill

I was lucky to have great parents and a great upbringing, which was interesting in all aspects. Abbeylands was a great house with wonderful memories. My first memories were going to school at home. In those days in some houses, before you went to National School, there was a lady called a governess, who was employed to teach the children of the house up to First Class. In the basement of Abbeylands was a room that I always knew as the school room. My first memories of going to the National School were of being dropped off by my Dad in some sort of jeep that he had at the time. Dr and Mrs May Holland were the teachers and they were great people, who taught three classes each.

The old school is still there but it is now a community building. There was a vegetable garden where the entrance of the tennis club is now, and to the right of the tennis club entrance there used to be a dry toilet – very primitive, I promise you. The playground stretched back to my father's land and along John McEvoy's field, which is now Central Park. When I got older I used to walk across the fields to school – great memories.

My memories of school are limited but strangely, the one memory I always have is of our class being looked after by an older boy who was very funny and who had us all laughing. That man was Liam Merriman, a great farming neighbour who is now gone to his Maker and whose family are still living in Richardstown. So when we youngsters were to be looked after in school we always wanted Liam.

The boys I remember when I was at school were George Manzor, Fergal Lee, Mick Corrigan, Hugh Corrigan, Seán Corrigan, Ned Cash, Declan Marron, the Curran family of Capdoo, as well as Paddy Bracken and the McManmon family, one of whom, Paddy, was in my class.

Clane in the early fifties was a very sleepy rural village of probably 200 to 300 people. Everybody knew everybody else and in later life that was the one sad thing about the changing times – we hardly know our next-door-neighbour, but that's what you call progress.

That time, you only played Gaelic football. If you played soccer, you were banned from Gaelic football. The season of 1954 was one not to be forgotten. Clane parish school team became the champions of Kildare. Tommy Merriman was the captain. I was lucky enough to be involved with that team. Seán Cribbin and Father Hughes were the trainers. Then we got a little older and we started playing soccer. My father gave the soccer club their first pitch where the entrance into Abbeylands Park is now, and where Damien O'Neill currently has his residence.

Charlie on Hunting Day in Clane, 1961.

They played there for a couple of years but, needing more space, Ned Shortt gave a field on the Dublin road. Our club was getting bigger and stronger and this was frowned upon by the GAA, which was worried that it was getting too strong. The goal posts were cut down one night but it only made the Clane Soccer Club stronger. Johnny Connolly of Connolly Construction and Brendan Mooney saved the day and eventually the soccer club moved down to my farm at Richardstown. We played there for maybe fifteen years and then the club bought its own pitches from the County Council on the Doctor's road, and went from strength to strength.

In the late forties and early fifties horses still played a big part on farms, and I suppose that is where my great love for horses, which is there to this day, was instilled in me. My first memories were of the work-horses on the farm, and being allowed to ride them in and out of the field.

Another memory was the Punchestown Races. Everybody went to the races, but the farm staff went in the Horse and Float, as it was called. I could have gone in the car, but no way – I went with the men and thought I was a big guy, what great memories, not realising that one day I would ride race horses there.

When I was maybe nine or ten, along with George Manzor, I built soap cars and raced them from outside the hall in Clane down the hill and in through the good gate behind the shop at Manzor's. You could do it then as there were very few cars on the road.

Another memory was when we started going to school to the Christian Brothers in Naas. We would all meet up and ride our bikes into school. Back then lorries were very slow, and

Clane soccer team in the early days, 1961. It included goalkeeper Seamus Manzor, George Manzor, Seán Delaney, and Tommy McManmon.

Strikers Colm and Edmond (Moll) Behan of Clane United.

Clane's first soccer team, 1957. Back row: Charlie Corrigan (manager), James (Son) Walsh, Seamus Manzor, Ned (Aggie) Cash, Peter Duffy, Seán (Sam) Corrigan. Front row: John (Chaw) Cash, Declan (Bodo) Marron, George Manzor, Michael Walsh, Jim Cash, Charlie O'Neill. This photograph was taken in Charlie O'Neill's field on the Celbridge road. The roundabout and Damien O'Neill's house are there now. Jimmy and Nanny Lecky's house is in the background.

along would come a lorry and one of the lads would ride fast, catch a hold of the lorry, and get towed into Naas – very dangerous. The best lads at this were Declan Marron and Hughie Corrigan. Fergal Lee and I had to try the same thing, but what happened? My father came along so all hell broke loose – what a thrill!

In those days, there was no door-to-door milk delivery, so everybody with a piece of land owned a cow, and in Clane village you had the parish priest, Father Doyle, the Presentation Sisters, John McEvoy, the Daly family, the Dunne family and Tommy Doyle who all lived on Main Street, all keeping cows. Every morning you would see the cows being walked down Main Street into the yard for milking – all families had one or two cows getting milked, making butter, getting buttermilk for making brown bread – all part of a simple way of living.

And so life went on and we came into the seventies and eighties and Clane started to become a dormitory village of Dublin. I suppose rural life died a little when we could no longer ride our horses through the village because of the increasing traffic. Also the new people of Clane (with no rural background) complained if there were horse droppings, but God help us, that's progress.

My parents bought Abbeylands in 1934 for £200, which was a lot of money then, as it was in the middle of the world recession. My parents and my uncle Charlie McConn had discovered that Abbeylands was for sale and they drove up the avenue to look at it with a view to buying it. On seeing Abbeylands for the first time, my mother fell in love with it and asked

The big double bank at Punchestown. 'I hope that ground is not too hard.'

my dad to buy it. So my father and uncle Charlie tossed on the step of Abbeylands to see which one of them would buy it. My dad won the toss and so he purchased it – what a way to buy a farm. Abbeylands was then owned by a Mr Penneran from England, whose daughter used to go to the village in a little pony trap pulled by a goat.

There is a great story about a ghost on the avenue of Abbeylands, told to me by Mick Archer, who worked for my dad during the war years. One wintry Sunday evening, Mick was coming up the avenue in the dark to feed the work-horses and coming to the bend in the avenue, under the big beech tree that is still there, he came on a man standing under it. He bid him the time and when he looked again the man was gone, as if he had disappeared into the tree. Mick Archer swore that this happened, so you can imagine; as a young man I always went by this tree very quickly, but I never saw anything.

In my early years of farming, my main enterprise was sheep-farming and one memory that always stands out was the sheep shearing. All the sheep used to come together on the farm at Abbeylands from our other farm at Richardstown – ewes and lambs totalling approximately 1,000. Driving these up or down the main road between Clane and Richardstown was a great sight. Drivers of cars would show great respect for the sheep and the herders, because that was the way rural Ireland operated. Nowadays you face the wrath of drivers, because everybody is in a hurry and under pressure. Those were the days in bygone Ireland. I wonder is the change for the better?

XII

GOALKEEPER, PHARMACIST, SINGER

Des Marron

I was born in 1934 in Lisdoonvarna, County Clare, where my father, Peter Marron, was stationed as a garda in Newmarket-on-Fergus. He had been moved, as was normal at the time, down along the West Coast, where he met my mother Brigid O'Connor in Castlegal, County Sligo. We moved to Clane in 1936 and I have been here ever since.

When I was about five years old I went to school. It was the custom at the time to go for one week to the Presentation Convent Sisters' school. All the boys were given a big welcome by Sister Joseph. On the first day she asked Aidan McGuinness (who was Garda McGuinness's son), 'Who made the world?' he correctly answered 'God made the world'. Being a bit forgetful, she asked him the same question the next day. Aiden replied 'Ah, shag it!! Didn't I tell you that yesterday?'

We moved down to the boys' primary school where we had a succession of teachers, ending up with Dr Holland. He was a Corkman and on a Monday morning, he would regularly entertain us with stories of the great hurler Christy Ring. He succeeded in giving us great insight into gardening by regularly taking the senior class into his large garden. And while we were about the various tasks he would hurl stones underhand at the nearby telephone pole. One day he nearly hit Lil Stanley as she went by on her bicycle, so she came into the school to complain, and he lined us all up and tried to find out who was the guilty party. My memories of school in those days were of warm, dusty roads, where we went barefoot and indulged in our favourite game with a bicycle wheel. This consisted of hurling the wheel in front of you as far as possible and spinning it back into your hand.

We also played home-made cricket in the Church Park, eleven-a-side. This game did not finish until about 11.00p.m. in those glorious summer evenings. Among the best players then were Séamus O'Donnell, affectionately known as 'Sod', Denis Kenny, the Harrington brothers and Larry Lee. I fancied myself as a left-hand bat and a right-hand fast bowler. At some stages in the game someone would hit the ball into Father Doyle's garden, and while hunting for the ball, we would inevitably rob the orchard. One must remember that in those days, prior to television, and with possibly only Radio Luxemburg and its star Pete Murry to listen to, one had to make up one's own games. One of those games, which may have been indigenous to Clane, was O'Grady Says. The redoubtable leader of O'Grady was Seamie Gill. Whatever O'Grady ordered you to do, it had to be obeyed, or else you faced a belt of a rod on your back. The other game was conkers. For the benefit of modern children who have never heard of this game: it consisted of picking up a large chestnut, putting a hole in it and inserting a piece of string about eighteen to twenty-four inches in length, then tying a knot at the end of the string and beating the living daylights out of your opponent's conker!

When we returned from the Christian Brothers' School Naas in the evenings, we played football on the streets of Clane. My father's gate next to the house was the goal. Up to twenty boys would kick the ball, which was an ordinary tennis ball, and try to score a goal. The crash of the ball hitting the galvanised gate was wonderful. Some of the Clane old-timers would come out of Jones' pub to watch the action. I remember Tom Parker, Harry Gill and Dinny Colgan, who used to tie up his ass outside the pub, regularly coming out to watch. In all the games we played I think we only broke one window in the courthouse next to the gate.

Time passed and I graduated in Pharmacy in 1959. I married Kathleen Fitzsimons, my present wife, as Hugh Leonard would put it! During the following years my wonderful family were born – Fiona, Marie, Victor, John, Kevin, and the twins Cecily and Edel. All this time and before, I played Under-14, Under-18, and senior football with Clane, and minor and senior football with County Kildare, the highlight being winning a Leinster Provincial Championship in 1956. When I retired in 1966 there was no active pursuit for a guy of thirty-three years. But in 1972 Bryan Sammon, Liam Burke Peter O'Neill and I, with the cooperation of Father Percy Winder (Clongowes Wood College), started a tennis club in Clongowes, and it became the success it is today. Later on, the club transferred to its current position in the schoolyard of the Clane boys' school. In the winter of 1972 Seamus Manzor said to me 'why not start a badminton club?' 'What's that?' said I. He said 'You hit a shuttle over a net and it is played indoors!' I replied 'Great, it sounds like winter-tennis'. And so it came about that Clane Badminton Club was formed.

I went to Elvery's Sports Shop in Dublin and bought two nets and a clatter of shuttles, and with the help of Edmond Behan, we used his big hall, which eventually had four courts, for the next ten to twenty-odd years. I served as chairman of both for about ten years.

In 1984, golf, which was always there, grabbed my attention, and is with me to the present day. I really enjoyed all my activities over the years including, KARE, Nás na Rí Singers, Clane Church choir, the Millicent Singers, Clane Musical Society, Clane Community Council and Clane Local Development, for which I act as secretary, and of course, my career as a pharmacist in my own lovely village … the village of Clane.

XIII

AS CLEVER AS A CAPDOO FOX

Father Michael Bracken

Capdoo was once very different from what it is today. There were only a few houses at both ends, and in the middle was O'Donnell's pond. It was widely regarded by the young people as a real test of courage to walk this area alone at night. It had no houses, a small pond, and was lined with high trees. Having done this walk I am not loath to confess that it was a fearful and sinister spot for us all and at times I simply ran for all I was worth until I got over McCreery's Hill and met the houses at the far side of it, namely Paddy Delaney's and Curran's. The hazardous part of this journey began with the houses of Joe Bibby and Peter O'Rourke, and it finished at Paddy Delaney's.

Both of these men, Joe Bibby and Paddy Delaney, were real characters and contributed much to what was the real Capdoo. Joe Bibby was almost unavoidable for anyone walking to or from Clane… everyone encountered him as he worked around his house on both sides of the road. He professed to know a lot about foxes, badgers, rodents, and other animals. He used to set snares for some of the predators that stole his chickens and hens.

One morning we were coming home from the early Sunday Mass and we passed O'Donnell's pond, where Joe was in top form. He had attracted a small crowd of onlookers with the news that he had caught a fox in his snares on the bank of the pond. Everyone was very excited to see this specimen, and Joe dutifully delayed the exhibition, milking it for what it was worth. Eventually, when all had assembled, he told the onlookers to stand back so he could go into the hedge and pull out the fox in the snare, which he dramatically did. We kids were afraid when we saw this big fox at such close quarters and backed off further, as did all the women and girls. Joe put the fox and snare down in the middle of the road, rubbed its coat, proclaimed that it was dead, and told us that we could all come closer and look at it, indeed feel it. Many did just that, to a continuous commentary from Joe on foxes and their ways. Not being satisfied with the number who had the courage to touch it, Joe took off the snare from its neck and invited more people to come closer, telling everyone it was dead and therefore perfectly harmless. So more did come to feel its coat and Joe was like a king with prize booty. Next thing, however, the fox jumped up and dived away into the ditch and it was gone! The people who had touched it were terrified to think that it had fooled all, including the expert Joe, and that it was fully alive as they touched it. Joe was totally deflated and the swears of him on this fox was really something to warm ears. Needless to say this fox dominated the conversations of Capdoo for a considerable time afterwards. All knew that even Joe had experienced something new in this fox. And we kids now understood the meaning of the saying '… as clever as a fox' – so clever it had brought about the public deflation of Joe!

Later, I myself saw a fox being chased by the hounds and the hunt coming from the direction of Higgins' farm. It crossed the river and as I watched it came across Shortt's field almost to our house, then carefully retraced its steps back into the river and moved away in the water. The hounds then arrived, crossed the river, and followed its scent to our house and were lost when the scent disappeared there.

To be in Capdoo was to be close to nature and to admire people like Joe who professed to know so much about its animals. Of course, we also lived on the meat of rabbits and catching these occupied not a small part of our time as children.

Paddy Delaney lived at the other end of the sinister spot of road. Paddy was a jack-of-all-trades and a cobbler. He was unmarried and when he got into a house there was a real problem about getting him out. He had no fixed time to begin work every day, so he got up when he felt like it. Thus he would stay till midnight or later in a house he went to mitch in. All sorts of ploys were tried to get him to go – without much success. Usually, members of a family would, one after another, just go to the bedroom and not come back. Those left would then realise their fate and attempt to steal away, leaving, eventually, one hapless soul stuck with Paddy past midnight! The rosary was known as a way of getting him to go.

Paddy's house was open to all the local children. All were made welcome and all did come to watch him soling a shoe and doing his work. He had a garden with nice apples and other fruits and we noticed that as Paddy was a night man, he never shaved till before he went out in the evenings. To shave he would put his mirror on the only back window in his cottage kitchen and in doing so he blocked out, for the time it took him to shave, the view to his garden. That was our moment: we stole his fruit as he shaved and did so without any danger or threat from Paddy. And even though he was known for his late-night visits, his house was the place where we would go and feel free to spend hours, there was never a time that Paddy would tell anyone to leave. And for children this was a unique experience, and it was a real part of the Capdoo culture.

XIV

HERE TO STAY

The Horan Family, Butterstream

Don't it always seem to go
That you don't know what you got till it's gone?
They paved paradise and put up a parking lot

The sweet melody of Joni Mitchell's song from the 1960s sums up the nostalgia that engulfs each one of our hearts as we now look down the Prosperous road in Clane. All those years ago, you could count on one hand the number of houses from the village to Firmount Cross. Now everything has 'changed, changed utterly'. Hindsight was not available to us as we lived our simple lives. We realise now our apparently simple lives were indeed special and unique. Times may change, as the opening lines imply, but precious memories never fade – memories we have passed on to our own children and some we wish to share with you now.

Joe and Máiread Horan with their four young children (the eldest just four years old) moved out to Clane from Walkinstown in Dublin in January 1954. Máiread never forgot that cold winter's evening and often spoke about it later to us. Her sister Breda moved out with them as their mother had passed away six weeks earlier. The truck with all their belongings pulled up on the side of the Prosperous road, outside a small thatched cottage which faced down towards the village. Máiread thought her life had ended. The whole place was in total darkness. Her first reaction was to want to jump back into the truck and drive back to Dublin but no, they were here to stay.

This was her first time to see the cottage, as Joe had been the only one to view it before this. He saw the ad in the evening paper: 'Thatched cottage for sale, with a few acres of land'. He jumped at the opportunity to buy the premises. He had always wanted to bring up his family in the country, as this was where he himself had been raised. He wanted a house with a little bit of land. He came from Ballycumber in County Offaly. Máiread came from Limerick Junction. He was a bus conductor in CIE, Conyngham Road garage, and Máiread was a receptionist in the hotels section in CIE. They met, married, lived in Walkinstown for a few years, and then the big opportunity of moving to Butterstream, Clane, arrived.

The first visitor to the door that evening was Bill Ennis, who just happened to be cycling up from the village. As he passed the Half-Mile Bridge, he heard a baby crying, and wondered what was going on. He noticed a light on in the thatched cottage – no one had lived here since Patsy Arnott had passed away. He went straight home first, and came back with a can of milk for the baby. The Ennis farm was in the field behind us and from that first meeting Ned

No penalty points then… The College road, Clane.

Murray's shop, Firmount.

and Bill Ennis became our very good friends and neighbours. The story of the baby was told so many times that people expected to hear it at all kinds of functions. It became Bill's party piece (along with 'She'll be coming round the mountain when she comes').

The cottage had no running water, two bedrooms, and one living room. A small glass-panelled window in the living room let in some light and gave a little view of the back of the house. A far cry from the three-bedroomed semi-detached house in Walkinstown! A big open fire welcomed you in the living room, where all the baking, cooking, heating of water and so on was done. The bathtub came out every Saturday evening, the water was heated, and one by one, we all had our weekly wash. The water was drawn from the pump at the Half-Mile Bridge. The buckets were all carried down in the morning and filled, and if needed were filled again in the evening. What a hard chore this was, but it had to be done daily.

The Horan family.

Shopping was another big task. The nearest shop to us was Miss White's (Murray's) at Firmount Cross. Nothing came pre-packed. Everything was weighed out as required: sugar, flour, oatmeal, rice, corn flour, sweets, etc. In those days, if you were lucky enough to have a halfpenny and asked for a halfpenny's worth of sweets, you would get a handful. As all the shopping was done locally, travelling to Dublin would be a very special treat or an occasional thing – maybe once a year! This might be at Christmas time.

Sunday afternoons were never spent indoors or wasted. This was the day when the matches were broadcast on the wireless. The day before a big match the battery would have been brought down to Wallace's Bicycle Shop on the main street to be charged up. We would all be sent off for a walk when the match was on. The walks would vary: it might be a stroll around Loughanure, a tour of Capdoo or maybe the Millicent road. We would be given maybe 2d (our Sunday treat) and we would not return until teatime. This would be safe time, as the match would be over then.

As we grew up, summers were spent making hay, thinning turnips, picking potatoes and cutting turf. We, like all families, were fairly self-sufficient. We grew our own potatoes and vegetables, had a cow and a few calves, a few pigs, hens, and ducks and were kept busy. Nevertheless, we still had time to play. All the families on the road would meet at the Half-Mile Bridge (about thirty in all). We played rounders, conkers, picked nuts from the trees in Ennis' field (the land where Clane Hospital and Hazel Hall Nursing Home now stand) and we climbed trees along the rampart. There was a little stream in the field where we loved to paddle and catch 'pinkeens'. We would be so proud carrying home our little jars of fish. There was a big hole in the middle of the field where we spent hours and hours playing. Every now and then, the 'townies' would arrive up from St Brigid's Terrace to challenge the Half-Mile Bridge gang, but they could never really master us.

Bedtime would be very early at night during the winter because there was nothing else to do. We would play games, cards and sing songs by candlelight. The biggest thing at night for the whole family was to say the rosary. Even the youngest in the family would have to kneel down

A day in the bog – Joe Horan, Lar
Casey, Jackie Cooper.

and pray. Máiread would commence the prayers and each one would take a turn at a decade of
the rosary. Any laughing or joking during this prayer-time would be frowned upon.

Máiread was a beautiful knitter and everything worn by us was knitted by her. She did not
have knitting patterns but made up her own designs. Breda was a dressmaker. They sat each night,
one sewing and the other knitting. The clicking of the knitting needles and the noise of the old
-fashioned sewing machine helped us drift off to sleep in the little bedroom next door.

Budget Travel or even Ryanair did not exist then, and the concept of booking a last-minute-
trip to the sun on the internet would have been completely alien to us. Holidays would be a day
trip to Glendalough with a picnic on the way home. We would all be dressed up in our Sunday
clothes for this outing. We looked forward to this trip from one year to the next. Another day out
(if we had time) was a trip to the zoo with another picnic on the way home. There was also a
visit to Ballycumber to see our granny and a chance to help out with the farming chores. During
the warm summer weather we spent our evenings swimming in the Liffey. All the families would
gather together and have a great time – the little ones paddling in the shallows and the older ones
out in the deep end. No worries back then about how clean the water was!

No one ever missed Mass. You would not be allowed. In fact, no one ever missed a church
ceremony. During Lent, we all went to Mass every morning at 8.00a.m., came home and got
ready for school. Most days we walked to church and back and then walked to school again,
it was something we all did. During the Easter ceremonies we were all marched down to the
church in our summer clothes. No one ever left the church early – you stayed for the rosary
and Benediction, and waited for the choir to finish the hymn. Good Friday was always a very
quiet day, and rhubarb tart was always on the menu on Good Friday.

Everyone back then started 'big' school between the age of three-and-a-half and four.
playschool or preschool was unheard of. Boys and girls started with the nuns in the old
convent school and when the boys made their First Holy Communion they moved down

Clane on tour – a day's outing in the sixties. From left to right: Ms Breda Fitzgerald, Jackie Cooper, Brendan Langan, John Tierney, Nan McCormack, Mrs Horan.

Cowboys at Punchestown: Joe Horan, Gerry Dunne, Pat Dunne, and John Tierney.

Right: Ned Ennis.

Below: Bill Ennis.

to the old boys' school on the Dublin road. The first exam we did was in sixth class. It was called the Primary Certificate. There was no secondary school in the village until the end of the sixties. Sister Perpetua, who had arrived in Clane in 1961, worked very hard along with Sister Lucy to get the Secondary Top started in 1969. Up until then you either went out to work after primary school or you travelled to Naas to the secondary or the Technical School, or went away to boarding school. Margaret, the eldest in our family, went on to boarding school in Mountmellick. She was also the first woman to apply for entry into Maynooth University.

Life seemed very simple then, but we enjoyed it all, and had some great laughs along the way. Ned Ennis was a great character and was known by everyone – a very intelligent man, we thought, as he always seemed to know so much about everyone and everything. He had a tradition in his house at Christmas while making the pudding. Nothing unusual about his recipe, but his secret was to get everyone who came into the house to stir the pudding bowl. That meant that every child on the Prosperous road had to take a turn. It seemed to go on for days. Then we all had a chance to taste it afterwards. He was also a great man for making pancakes. Ned and Bill were at every function in every house on the road and had a party piece for all occasions. They were wonderful characters – there wasn't a household on the Prosperous road that hadn't Ned or Bill as godparent to one of their children.

Another great memory was helping Paddy and Mick Gill in Butterstream with the bringing home of the hay. We all gave a hand at stacking the hay. When it came to drawing it home, we all took turns at sitting on the back of the bogie. The summers always seemed to be filled with long, sunny days. We will never forget the day Gill's hay barn went on fire. The fire brigade arrived from Naas and used the water from the stream alongside their house to put out the fire. As the stream emptied we could see the eels trying to float around. Ned Ennis came along with a bucket and caught the eels, brought them all home, put the butter in the pan and threw the eels on to it. What a feast he had that day!

Another great character was Kate Kearney. She lived in a little cottage where the GAA Clubhouse is now. She kept lots of hens, ducks, and other animals. A visit to Kate Kearney's cottage on the way home from Mass or church ceremonies was quite common.

Life moved on and things changed. We now had ten children in our family, three boys and seven girls. Joe had become a bus inspector in CIE, we moved to decimals and left behind the shillings and pence, and the first television came into our house in the mid-sixties. We watched and loved programmes like *The Virginian*, *Lassie*, and *Mister Ed*, all in black and white. The outside world was now open to us. The old thatched cottage was knocked to the ground and a three-bedroomed detached bungalow built in its place. We no longer carried buckets to the pump at the Half-Mile Bridge. We had a secondary school in the village. The population of Clane was increasing. More houses were built on the Prosperous road.

On reflection, we realise now how sweet Joni Mitchell's melody is and the words 'you don't know what you got, till it's gone' have a very true meaning for all of us who lived on the Prosperous road all those wonderful years ago. As William Wordsworth so succinctly put it:

> Bliss was it in that dawn to be alive,
> But to be young was very heaven.

XV

SAM CORRIGAN, FOOTBALL AND SOUR APPLES

Jim Byrne

The Clane I grew up in – what memories that uncovers. I will stay clear of buildings and the changes involved, I am sure others will have them well covered. One of the things that comes to mind right away was how lucky I felt if I got the price of a few sweets, but it did not matter much, as every other lad was in the same boat.

Going to school there was a sort of unofficial divide between the townies and the country lads. This led to some great Loughanure versus the Terrace football games. The Terrace had the upper hand seventy per cent of the time, but one game sticks out, played in our home ground (Ennis's field at the Half-Mile Bridge). We had what we reckoned was a good team, and then our secret weapon stepped forward in the shape of the referee for the game, Sam Corrigan. Every ball anywhere near the Terrace goal: 'Penalty to Loughanure'. We won that one.

When I think of how simply we got our enjoyment, hunting rabbits for hours on end with dogs that would not catch a cold. I think the rabbits felt sorry for us and would pop up and give us a chase every so often. Potato- and fruit-picking in Clongowes Wood College played a big part in our lives and many a young lad was dressed for the coming year through the results of their labour. At the end of the school year, when the students' lockers were cleared out of boots, jerseys, socks, etc., if you had a bit of inside information about when this clearance was due to happen, you could have your pick.

Various other things come to mind – the first Saturday of every month, wash behind your ears and get down that road to Confession, fasting from the night before and setting off home after Mass on a Sunday morning, there were only two houses between the village and our house, McCormack's and Dr Walsh's. I still drool when I think of the smell of rashers, sausages, and eggs wafting out through the open window of Nan McCormack's as we passed, God rest you, you never knew the spring you put in our step, hunger was great sauce, the plate would be lucky to survive when we made it home.

A small story about how innocent we were: one of our family arrived home one Saturday morning with a lovely turnip under his arm. 'Look what I brought you home for the dinner Ma!' After a couple of shouts, a thump or two, and the usual refrain 'Do you mean to tell me you robbed this on your way home from Confession?' 'No Ma I got it on the way down, hid it in the hedge, told the priest, and collected it on the way home.' I was out in the next field and did not see the reaction.

Clane was always steeped in GAA, and even though it was quite a while since a Cummins Cup came to the village hopes were always high. For all of us snotty-nosed articles of the late

The boys' football team – with captain Jim Byrne in the centre with the ball – with Woods garage in the background. Back row: Tony Doherty, Stan McManmon, Pat Mulhall, John Mulhall, Michael Gibbons, ? , Pat Timmons, Tim O'Brien, Robbie Booth. Front row: Cecil Dunne, Christo McCormack, Noel McManmon, Jim Byrne, Frank Behan, Pat Burke, Tony Langan.

fifties, the way to the games was in Kit Walsh's lorry. Kilcock was the team of that era with big names like Moran, McCormack, Dalton and the Gibbons brothers, names we only heard on the radio while our head were stuck through the window of Paddy Lavin's shop. To stand in Hazelhatch and watch the draw and replay, and see those icons in the flesh was something no young GAA man could forget. I think Pat Griffin played his last championship game for Clane in one of those exciting encounters in 1962.

Young boys will always find ways to amuse themselves. Football, shooting at birds with a catapult – I shudder when I think of that – the only saving grace is that I can't remember killing one. High on the list of amusements were all orchards in the area – God, some of the apples tasted more like lemons. One in particular springs to mind: running across the church parks at lunch break and into Mr Marron's orchard, we were afraid of our lives of the big sows he had in the garden. Why we went in in the first place is beyond me – the apples were the same colour as Robin Hood's uniform, and as big as a small turnip. I swear the poor auld sow's eyes watered when she bit one.

As time passed, secondary school, work, marriage and family would become our main focus, and rightly so, but those memories will always remain clear and very important.

Our heartfelt regrets, to Monica and family especially, as Jim is no longer physically with us. But we are sure that his wit and personality live on in his heavenly home.
The authors

XVI

GROWING UP IN MAINHAM, c.1945 – 1955

Denis Dunne

Having been born in the late thirties, I shall try to write down some recollections of Mainham from approximately the mid-forties to the mid fifties. The focal points in Mainham then, and indeed well before, were the Royal Oak Bar and grocery shop, the forge, and the post office. I grew up at the forge. Mainham was a great place to grow up in as far as I was concerned. Like most of the families around here, on the one hand we had very little, but at the same time we lacked for nothing. Hard manual work was the order of the day. It is impossible to write about Mainham without intertwining it with Clongowes Wood. Practically every household had at least one, if not two people working in Clongowes, and those not directly making a living from it did so indirectly. For example, Clongowes farm had about thirteen work-horses and a few ponies, all of which were shod in the forge, not to mention repairing ploughs, harrows, grubbers, bogeys, dray wheel, etc. There were also a car and lorry for hire at the forge. Tom Murphy from Mountarmstrong drove the lorry and my father usually drove the car. During the war years Clongowes provided quite a lot of the business for the car and lorry.

The Second World War, which was known as the Emergency here, was from 1939 to 1945. The war meant very little to us as children, but it did mean something to our parents. Most foods were rationed. Coupons were supplied by the government, and these entitled each household, depending on the number in it, to buy a certain quantity of tea, sugar, butter etc. Petrol was also rationed, and it was well-nigh impossible to buy a tube or a tyre for a bicycle. The coupons were always kept on the top shelf of the kitchen dresser in our house, out of harm's way.

I started school at the age of five in the old convent school with some other boys from Mainham and, after First Holy Communion at the age of seven, moved to the boys' school on the Dublin road. In the boys' school Mrs Holland taught up to second class and her husband, Dr John Holland, taught from third class up. Some children from Mainham went to Prosperous school.

For First Holy Communion you were decked out in a new suit, which was taken off when you came home from Mass and was kept for Sunday-wear only, and it was handed down when you outgrew it. There was no such thing then as booking a table in a hotel for a meal, or indeed having your photo taken, as practically no one had a camera. You were lucky if you got a few bob from close relatives.

The Woods Centre, Hillview, St Brigid's Terrace, Hillview Heights, Loughbollard, and all the other housing areas were just green fields with cattle or sheep grazing on them at that time.

Clane school – only fifty students attended the school at this time.

In fact, Loughbollard, which was owned by Jim Manzor, was the GAA football field. In a wet winter a large pond would appear in the field and I remember on the way home from school often counting the number of seagulls and swans swimming in it. There were approximately sixty pupils on the roll-call in the boys' school from 1944 to 1949 and I think a similar number of girls in the convent. Part of our curriculum in the boys' school was digging and planting the garden, which ran alongside the road. If some fellow we knew was walking along the road we would pelt him with clods – provided, of course, Dr Holland was not about.

A regular job during the week before Christmas in our house, indeed in many houses throughout Ireland, was the parcelling up of a turkey to send to a relative in England. Apparently turkeys were as scarce as hens' teeth during and for some years after the war. The parcelling was not difficult, but trying to get the naggin of whiskey into the turkey where you put the stuffing was tricky. Our turkey was posted to our aunt and her family in the Isle of Wight. Officially the post office would not accept a parcel exceeding thirteen pounds in weight but, since another aunt was postmistress, a blind eye was turned if ours exceeded the maximum weight.

The week before Christmas the Clane GAA Club and Dramatic Class presented a play and concert in the gymnasium in Clongowes. This was inaugurated in 1947 and continued annually for eighteen years. The first year *Boolavogue* was presented, and the second year *Knocknagow*. Some local talent was usually in the concert, as well as comedians and singers from Dublin. Jack Cruise and Kevin Hilton were among these.

Boys from Mainham served as altar boys in the People's Church in Clongowes. One usually joined when one was nine or ten and retired when one got into long trousers at the age of thirteen. There were seven of us as altar boys during my four years from 1946 to 1950. There were between thirty-five and forty priests resident in Clongowes then, as well as five or six Brothers.

When the students went home on holidays at Christmas, Easter and Summer times, we went down at 8.00a.m. each morning to serve three Masses. There were three altars in the People's Church, four in the Students' Church and one in the castle, with Masses celebrated at the same time at each altar. After serving the three Masses we would go into the staff dining hall and be served with a boiled or fried egg, two slices of toast and a mug of tea. On Christmas morning we would serve nine Masses, as each priest celebrated three Masses on that morning. The Mass was in Latin then and the priest had his back to the congregation the whole time, even at the consecration. Even though we learned the Latin responses off by heart we hadn't a clue what they meant.

We always looked forward to the week after Christmas when Brother McEntee, who had the patience of Job, would take the altar servers to a pantomime in Dublin. Mick Holligan would drive us to Maynooth in the College van. Then there would be a scramble to get into the top front seats in the double-decker bus. When we reached Dublin, Brother McEntee would take us to Henry Street and let us loose in Woolworth's store for about an hour, and then on to the Monument Café in O'Connell Street for dinner. After dinner, we were off to either the Olympia in Dame Street or the Gaiety Theatre off Grafton Street. Jimmy O'Dea and Maureen Potter would be performing in the Gaiety and Jack Cruise in the Olympia. It was always dark when we came out of the theatre. Then we were taken to some restaurant for tea and after that to the double-deck bus and back to Maynooth where Mick Holligan, with the van, was always waiting to meet us. Were it not for Brother McEntee I doubt if any of us would have had the opportunity of seeing a pantomime in Dublin.

On St Stephen's Day some of us would dress up and go out with the wren. None of us could play a musical instrument so instead we would sing the usual song –

> The wren the wren the king of all birds
> On St Stephen's Day it was caught in the furze
> Up with the kettle down with the pan
> Give us a penny to bury the wren.

We usually got a piece of Christmas cake or pudding. Money was very scarce but the odd time we would get a few coppers.

Hunting rabbits during the winter months was very popular with us youngsters. Joe Conneff from Betaghstown brought us a lovely little pup one evening. It was so small he had it in his coat pocket. It turned out a lovely friendly mongrel terrier but if it saw a rabbit it would go through fire and brimstone to catch it. On Saturday mornings we usually went hunting rabbits and when we came home at dinnertime some other young neighbours would be waiting to take the terrier out again. Seldom, if ever, did we come home empty-handed. During the war- and post-war years rabbit was on the dinner menu in most households once or twice a week. Boiled or fried rabbit was nice and tasty.

Early every January the stream on the College front (cow) lawn where part of the golf course is would be dammed and within a week a large pond covering an area of approximately three acres would form. Within a few days it would freeze up and remain so for 3 weeks, if not longer. The winters were much colder then than now. Every day after school we would go sliding on the pond. The boy with the hob-nailed boots would slide the furthest. The College students and some priests all had proper skates that they clipped onto their boots. They would play an ice hockey match using coats or jerseys as goal posts. At the end of the game they would speed around the perimeter of the pond as you see on TV.

I always looked forward to St Patrick's Day. Mrs O'Haran from the Royal Oak, who had a car, always took her two sons Billy and Paddy, and myself, to Dublin to see the parade and then on to Croke Park for the Railway Cup finals. We usually watched the parade from the upstairs window of Clery's restaurant, which overlooked the GPO. The parade would pass by in fifteen minutes or so, as it only consisted of soldiers marching and a few tanks and armoured cars. At Croke Park up to 40,000 people used to attend the Railway Cup finals. Munster was usually in the hurling final and it was in these games that I saw the legendary Christy Ring play. Anytime he got the ball, a buzz would go up in the crowd. A feature of St Patrick's Day then was that everyone, and I mean everyone, wore a sprig of shamrock or at least a green badge.

During the winter there were films shown nearly every week in Clongowes gym for the students. They were usually shown on Wednesday nights, but sometimes on other nights. One way or the other, by bush telegraph, we would always hear in advance. We would troop down early and sit on the benches or gym horses at the back of the gym. Then the students would enter. They had ordinary wooden chairs to sit on. Then about twenty priests or so would come in and they sat on nice upholstered chairs at the back of the students and just in front of us. The rector sat on what looked like a mini-throne. As the priests entered the students went silent and stood to attention. Then the lights would be switched off and the film would start. Father Joe Kelly was usually the projectionist and sometimes Father McGlade or Father O'Byrne. The films were all in black and white then. Jimmy Durante was a regular, but the best were the cowboy films, especially those with Hopalong Cassidy and his sidekick Gabby Hayes. The only actress I remember was Deanna Durbin because she was a good singer. After about an hour there would be a break of three minutes or so to put a new reel in the projector. At the end of the film the student's captain would stand up and shout three cheers for Father Rector – hip hip hooray. By the time of the last hooray we'd be on our way out the back door of the gym to thread our cold, dark and sometimes wet way up the front avenue.

Clongowes was also a great source of comics, especially the *Beano* and the *Dandy*. They were obviously collected in the junior students' dormitory and placed in an area near the courtyard that housed the laundry, dairy and tailor's shop, awaiting collection for the dump in the farm field called the Clump. But sometimes before they were collected we got to them. Having read them we would take them to school in Clane and sell them to the Clane boys for a 1d. for three. They were great value for the buyer and a source of income for the seller. After all, a penny at that time would buy a bar of chocolate or a handful of bull's-eyes or Liquorice Allsorts from the big glass jars that the shopkeepers had on the counter – or indeed two Woodbines. However, the Clane boys soon found out the source of our comics and got to them before us. This resulted in a serious loss of revenue for us.

Easter was usually a quiet time in Mainham. However, we altar boys were usually busy with the Good Friday ceremonies and the Masses on Easter Sunday morning. One Easter Monday I was taken to see the Irish Grand National at Fairyhouse, but that time I was more interested in all the razzmatazz amusements there than watching the horses.

In 1949 I received confirmation. It was in Clane once every three years, usually in March. Pupils from Rathcoffey, Staplestown, Tiermohan, as well as Clane all gathered for the big day. Dr Keogh, Bishop of Kildare and Leighlin, would be accompanied in the church by Father Doyle

PP and the two curates. They would arrive at 10.30a.m. in the church and ask every boy and girl a question on the catechism. We were well tutored in the catechism by Dr Holland, but whether it was because we were in awe of or indeed afraid of the bishop and the parish priest, we had difficulty in spluttering out an answer. It was a great relief when you heard him say 'next'. It would take about two hours for the bishop to ask all the boys and girls a question on the catechism. Then they would retire to the parish priest's house where the housekeeper would have something for them to eat. Jones's grocery shop always got in extra buns and lemonade for that day and that's where we headed. At 2.00p.m. we would reassemble in the church. Dr Holland acted as sponsor for the Clane boys and he insisted that we all took the name Conleth for confirmation. St Conleth, together with St Brigid, are the joint patron saints of Kildare. I am told the nuns insisted that each girl took either Mary or Brigid. If you were called Mary then you took Brigid and if you were called Brigid you took Mary. I don't know what happened if you were christened Mary Brigid. Like the First Holy Communion there was no such thing then as hotel tables being reserved or photos taken, just straight home and into your old clothes.

Springtime was a very busy time in Mainham. Practically every house had a garden of some size or other. The garden was dug and planted with all kinds of vegetables and potatoes. Jim and Peter Connolly, in my opinion, had the best-kept garden in our area. Also in the forties and fifties there was no such thing as bottled milk being delivered. Those houses with someone working in Clongowes brought home their little can of milk each evening from the dairy or farm there. The rest of us would keep a cow in a local farmer's field. Our cow was kept in Peter Coonan's field. The cow was out both day and night in the summer and my mother would go to the field both morning and evening with her enamel bucket and milk it. In winter it was brought home each evening and was housed in a small shed and it would be milked there. When the cow calved we always bought a second calf as the cow gave enough milk for the household and to feed both calves. When the calves were weaned they were tied out on the green to graze and at the age of one year were sold.

Punchestown Races always followed Easter at the end of April. It was a two-day meeting back then, Tuesday and Wednesday, and it meant two days holiday from school. The week before Punchestown those with whitewash on the walls of their houses would renew the whitewash, paint the windows and doors and generally freshen up the place. This was a tradition in Mainham. During the war years and indeed for a year after it, the Cosgrave family from near Enfield walked their three or four racehorses to Punchestown on the Sunday before. The grooms always stopped at the Royal Oak for a drink and of course always assured us that the horses would win. Sometimes one or two did. On the Tuesday morning we got our bicycles ready and joined up with groups of cyclists from Rathcoffey or Donadea or even Kilcock. We always headed for the free area opposite the stands on the course, indeed most people did. There was every kind of amusements there as well as the usual tote and bookies. In the late forties I remember seeing a tall black man, dressed in flamboyant robes and headdress with about 100 various coloured small bottles of liquid selling at 1s each. They were to cure arthritis, lumbago, sciatica, headache and so on. Soon they were all gone, and so was he.

Everyone looked forward to summer – holidays, football, swimming and the chance to earn a few bob. During the late forties we were able to muster ten or twelve lads between the ages of nine and thirteen to play football. Two teams of five or six would be picked and we played the matches either in Coonan's field opposite the Royal Oak or in Farrell's field behind Smyth's.

Sometimes these turned out to be tense and tempers became frayed. When playing in Farrell's field, Eugene Smyth came out and refereed them and at the same time helped keep the peace. It was at these games that Pa Connolly cut his teeth, as it were. Pa later represented Clane and Kildare minors and seniors for many years and in 1965 was selected on the Ireland football team that played an American selection in the Cardinal Cushing games in New York. I remember on about two occasions around 1948, on Saturday mornings, with approximately eight or nine lads we played a similar Clane team in a small field that is now Hillview, using coats as goalposts and without a referee. We would have arranged these matches in the school on the Friday evening. Our battle cry as we took the field was 'Eggs and rashers for the Mainham Dashers, hay and oats for the Clane goats'. I often wondered why the Clane lads walloped us!!

In Clane at that time there was only the GAA football club with no clubhouse, as there is now. There was no soccer, rugby, tennis, badminton or golf clubs either. In the early fifties a boxing club was formed by Father Hughes CC, and the trainer was Mr Clancy who ran a shop near the abbey. I remember attending a few boxing shows in the old hall and one in Clongowes gym. In the late fifties a cycling club was formed in Clane called United Road Club, and its members took part in all the cycling events throughout Leinster and elsewhere. We usually went to the football field in Loughbollard on a Sunday to watch the matches. That time there were no dressing rooms, so the members of the opposing teams would tog out at opposite corners at the far end of the field. When the referee blew for half-time, all the supporters of each team would go to the middle of the field to give advice to the players. This was also the signal for Mr Ford of Naas to trot his pony and dray, which was filled with oranges and minerals, to the centre of the field where the supporters would buy the players a mineral or orange to quench their thirst. Then when the referee would signal the start of the second half, Mr Ford would trot his pony and dray back behind the goalposts to continue

Three little angels – the First Holy Communion group.

selling his wares and the supporters would return to the sidelines. No match was complete in Clane without Bill Molloy, the ould stunt, playing his melodeon up and down each sideline singing 'The good old hills of Carbury' and collecting a few coppers. Ike Keogh from Naas was another regular, minding the bicycles. We loved seeing Cappagh play Ardclough as there was usually a bit of aggro before the end.

In July we never missed the opportunity to take trips on the Clongowes farm bogeys as they brought the cocks of hay from the various fields to the farmyard. Coming to the end of August was always mushroom time. Unlike now, nearly every field had mushrooms. The two best fields were the Brick field in Clongowes, and Farrell's big field beside Downey's land. Often I arrived in these fields at about 6.30a.m. only to find a half dozen neighbours there before me with their cans or paper bags or traneens laden with mushrooms. But as soon as the mushrooms were picked, others appeared in their place. Anyway, there was more than enough for everyone. Back home, having prepared them, one could either boil them in milk, fry them on the pan, or roast them on the hearth, always of course with a pinch of salt and pepper. They were delicious. The wild mushrooms that time were far superior in taste and flavour to the modern mushroom grown in the tunnel.

In September after school we would hear at which local farmer's haggard the threshing machine was working and we would head there. It was nearly always White's thresher pulled by a steam engine, which Harry Timmons sometimes drove. There would be two men on the reek tossing the sheaves to the top of the thresher, where two more would cut the binding and drop them into the drum. At one end of the thresher the grain would come out into the sacks, the other end the straw, and at the middle the chaff. One man kept replacing the full sacks, one kept cleaning the chaff and three or four or more kept removing the straw and forming a reek. The modern combine harvester has now replaced the wonderful old threshing machine.

Father Bob Thompson driving a tractor in Clongowes Wood College.

Threshing in Castlebrown, Clane. The group includes Joe Higgins, John Higgins, Lar Higgins, Brigid Higgins, Ned Shortt, Pat Shortt, Peter Shortt, Paddy Delaney, Pat Timmons, Michael Murphy, and Johnny Nevin.

Prize bulls at Clongowes Wood College. Included in the picture are Tom and Frank Smyth.

We swam in both the Gollymochy in Coonan's field and the Liffey. In the Gollymochy we'd build a dam to raise the water level high enough, but the Liffey was much much better. At that time the Liffey water was crystal clear, unpolluted, and with an abundance of fish, especially trout. To reach the Liffey we'd cycle through Capdoo and leave the bicycles at Shortt's house. Then we'd walk across two fields. The fast-flowing water was great to swim in.

To earn the few bob we got piece-work picking fruit in the walled garden at Clongowes or tinning turnips or mangolds in a field at the farm. We earned our pocket money this way and it kept us out of harm's way.

Every autumn in the forties, the horse-drawn circus arrived for one night to the green in Mainham. It usually arrived around noon and within a short time the big top would be erected and everything was ready for the show that night. There were the usual clowns, trapeze artists, performing dogs, ponies, monkeys, and sometimes lions. The following morning there wouldn't be sight or light of anything left on the green – all gone to their next venue.

At Halloween four or five of us would go out on the Pooka. We would dress up in old clothes and masks and call to houses singing some song or other. We never came back empty-handed, usually got apples and nuts, and it was a good bit of fun. Then there was the usual games of trying to bite an apple as it swung around on a piece of string or trying to fish a coin out of a basin full of water with your mouth.

In 1949-50 most of us were about to finish National School. As there was no secondary school in Clane then, nor indeed was there any talk of one being established, most of us went to the Christian Brothers' secondary school in Naas, some went to the Technical School in Prosperous and indeed two or three went to boarding school. We cycled to Naas every day in a group and it took about three quarters of an hour. The only time it was tough was when it rained all the way in and our clothes were wet all day and then we had to put on the wet top coat, which seemed to weigh a ton coming home. The school was situated behind Marum's pub beside the town hall. It is now the Moat Theatre. In 1955 the Leaving Certificate class consisted of just ten pupils – three from Naas, two from Mainham, one from Clane, one from Dunlavin, one from Sherlockstown, one from Killashee and one from Kill. There was no continental language, such as French, German or Spanish, taught in the school, only Latin. It used to be said that Latin was taught just in case some of the students went on to study for the priesthood.

Just before Christmas 1952 one of the two greatest things to hit Mainham happened – it was, of course, rural electrification. The other great thing, mains water, arrived about nine years later. Before the electricity poles were erected, rumours began to circulate about how dangerous it was; one rumour was that anyone with a thatched house shouldn't get it as it was likely to set the thatch on fire. When it eventually arrived, everyone, even those with thatched houses, got connected up. It was great. No more having to do the school lessons under the flickering oil lamp or candle, no more trying to get into bed in a dark room, not being able to find a candle. No longer trying to save the wet and dry wireless batteries during the week in order that they would last out listening to Mícheál O'Hehir broadcast the big match on Sunday. Now at the flick of a switch the whole house lit up. The electric radio arrived and out went the wireless, batteries and all. By degrees the electric kettle, cooker, fridge etc. began to appear and you wondered how on earth you lived before electricity.

In 1953, 1954 and 1955, during the three-month summer holidays, about five or six of us from Mainham got employment harvesting turf, or footing turf as it was called, in the Bórd na Móna bog in Timahoe. We would leave home at 7.00a.m. each morning and cycle via Prosperous, turn right at Dag Weld's pub and over the Canal bridge (no longer there) and then by the grand new housing estate at Coill Dubh. The train departed the works at 8.00a.m. and the six or so wagons would be packed to capacity with locals and a large number who lived in the billets at the Timahoe camp. There were over twenty trenches out the bog, and the train would stop at whichever trenches the turf was fit for footing. It was piece-work, and the harder you worked, the more you earned.

For the first week it was hard on the back and hands, but then you got used to it. We brewed up at 11.00a.m. and 3.00p.m. each day and the craic was always good around the fire. It was lovely and peaceful out in the bog and the only sound was that of the skylark and of course the crows. The same crows left many a worker without his evening lunch if he forgot to zip up his lunch bag after the morning break. At 5.30p.m. the train came again and collected all the workers at the trenches and brought them back to the works. We then cycled home and arrived shortly before 7.00p.m. We met plenty of young men from the western seaboard there who hadn't got the through fare from the west to England. They would work for three weeks or a month there and save up enough money to buy the boat and train ticket to cover the onward journey to Britain.

Joe Corr, a native of Howth, who lived opposite Paddy Lavin's grocery shop, now McKenna's Hardware, was the postman. He left Clane every morning at 9.00a.m. with his satchel of letters and travelled up the Ballinagappagh road, Betaghstown, Ballynaboley and always arrived at the Forge in Mainham at 10.00a.m. Irrespective of whether he had letters or not he always called to the forge. There were two reasons for that. One was that he brought the *Irish Press* from Miss Reddy's thatched newsagent's shop in Clane to the forge, and the other was that he put his billycan on the forge fire and brewed up his mug of tea. He would sit on the bench and eat his sandwich, drink his tea, and after that light a cigarette and read the paper. The forge was a good place for a story or two and Joe brought the latest news from Clane.

Prior to and during the war-years, Boland's bread was transported by rail from Dublin to Sallins rail station and picked up there by Peter Shortt and Mr Slevin, who both had Boland's horse-drawn bread vans. Peter's route on Mondays, Wednesdays and Fridays took him via Clane to Mainham, where he supplied bread to his customers at their doors, and also to shops including the Royal Oak. Because his horse did so much road-work he had to have his hooves re-shod every week in Mainham forge, and in icy conditions special studs were fitted to the horse-shoes to help keep him from slipping.

Something that I miss very much now, and that was taken for granted in the forties, is the sound of the singing birds. There were at least twenty times more thrushes, blackbirds, goldfinches, chaffinches, wrens, robins, yellow hammers, linnets and other birds than the meagre few there are now. Early on spring and summer mornings the lovely sound of not one but several thrushes singing intermingled with chirping of the finches, and was a joy to wake up to. In the springtime, no matter what hedgerow you looked at, there were lots and lots of birds' nests, unlike now. During the day all the birds were fluttering here and there, foraging for food. In the late summer evenings, when the birds had settled in the hedges for the night, along would come a kestrel looking for its supper, which it usually got, and the crescendo of frenzied noise from the small birds trying to drive the intruder away is a sound that remains with one for a long time. It must be thirty years or more since I've seen or heard the corncrake in the meadows, not to mention the cuckoo. The only species which seem to have survived in numbers are the crow family and the scrounging magpies which systematically trawl the hedgerows in spring to kill the young birds in the nests. Also completely disappeared are the beautiful timid red squirrels, only to be replaced by the obnoxious grey squirrel, which some people describe as a rat with a furry tail. The grey squirrels are responsible for eating the bark off young trees, especially beech, which subsequently die.

As I mentioned earlier, practically every household had a cabbage garden in the forties, but not now, and also every household kept a few hens. We usually kept a dozen or so various breeds – Rhode Island Reds, Black Minorcas and White Wyandottes. Every summer one would temporarily disappear and three weeks later reappear with about a dozen chicks trotting after her. She was so protective of her chicks, especially when a kestrel or rat appeared and tried to nick one. How times change, I don't think there is one house in Mainham now that keeps hens. Pity, because the taste of a free-range egg is so much nicer than the battery one.

Mainham has changed in the last fifty-five years, from a few cars chugging by daily, to hundreds speeding by on the new road that was completed in the year 2000. The old thatch and whitewash-walled houses are gone and replaced by nice new houses, all for the better.

I don't know who penned the following poem but I think it is appropriate for the forge in Mainham:

> Closed is the door, the Forge is no more
> And it makes sad rural news
> For the blacksmith sang and his anvil rang
> When he made the horses' shoes
> The visiting fellows used blow his bellows
> As the tested on animals hoof
> While his farmer friend a hand would lend
> Or sometimes stand aloof
> The horse and mare were his daily care
> As he plied his steady trade
> Early or late to repair a gate
> Or even 'let in' a spade
> And here the elite were wont to meet
> And plans made mid the noise
> As was done before in days of yore
> By Wexford's Croppy boys

I have named below the families living in the houses, some unoccupied, circa 1945. Starting at Capolis Road (Clongowes back avenue) to the Dog's Hill, which is about 300 yards on the cemetery side of Borehole crossroads. The Dog's Hill was levelled when the new road was constructed in 2000:

Kearys
Unoccupied, later Holligans
Connollys
Paddy Connolly
Cribbins
Murphys
Smyths
Downeys
Dunne's post office
Gunner Delaney, later Rourkes
O'Haran's Royal Oak
Delaneys
Dunne's forge
Byrnes
Unoccupied, now Boland's
Timmons
Moloneys, later Jim Timmons
George Delaney
Unoccupied, later Julia Graham and Rose Wing
Grahams
Walshs
Coonans, now Wyles
Cribbins
Moloneys

I wish to acknowledge the major contribution made to this article by Seán Cribbin.

Denis

XVII

LETTER FROM ZIMBABWE

Sister Perpetua

It is both a privilege and a pleasure to include my memories in this book, as I shall never forget the people of Clane and the surrounding parishes.

It is the Lord who assigned me to the primary school in Clane in 1961. Shortly after my arrival I experienced wonderful people who were most generous and willing to help me. Since then it has been a great joy to have shared life with my Presentation Sisters and to have worked in the primary and secondary schools. The unparalleled support and help I received entailed fundraising over a long period as the people realised that there was no substitute for education. I recall the countless sacrifices that were made to repair the old primary school, to rebuild the courthouse, erect extra classrooms on the convent campus, and the pre-fabricated classrooms on the Prosperous road. We would not have qualified for a grant for the present new buildings if we had not erected the extra classrooms.

I take this opportunity to thank the Sisters, priests, the dedicated staff and all the people of Clane and the surrounding areas for their unsurpassed support, generosity and kindness shown to me during my very happy years in Clane. I wish to thank my generous and caring past pupils, their parents and others in the Clane area, who have supported and continued to support financially my mission in Zimbabwe since 1982. They have funded the education of young adults who are extremely poor. I prepare them for a public examination and it is a joy to teach them. Letters I have received from past pupils have assured me that apart from receiving an excellent education they have never failed to attend Sunday Mass. They have told me that their appreciation of the Eucharist and a deepening of their faith are due to the religious instruction they received in Scoil Mhuire. This has given me great joy as a deep faith is their greatest treasure in life.

I recall with gratitude the support of my dear Sisters who have gone to God. I wish Sister Dominica and the present staff every success and blessing as they continue the good work in Clane.

First students in the school. Back row: S. Holligan, M. Walshe, M. Reilly, P. Corrigan, E. Higgins, M. Donagher, B. Leonard, M. Leonard, M. O'Connor. Front row: H. Coughlan, M. Murphy, S. McCormack, R. McCormack, A. McCormack, M. Geraghty, A. Keary.

The official opening of Scoil Mhuire, 1984: Marie O'Rourke, Father James Dalton, Garda Pat Walsh, Martha Daly, Councillor Seán Reilly, Mary Donohue, Moira O'Shaughnessy, Garda Noel Cummiskey, Father Pat Hennessy.

Sister Perpetua and Sister Dominica planting an oak tree outside the new community school in May 1984.

Sister Perpetua's walk.

Tom and Mrs McEvoy.

XVIII

FROM CLANE HALL TO KILMURRY BOG

Tony McEvoy

We came to Clane in 1948, when I was nine years old. Our first trip to view the house that my father was interested in buying was probably in March. The house was Kearns', beside the old hall on the College Road. The only thing I remember about that day was my brother and I watching with fascination as a young Kearns boy of about our own age sat outside the front door while our father and mother were inside talking to his parents. He was using a hatchet to chop a wooden hand grip off a front-loading flintlock pistol which he told us he had found in the back field. It was years before I was to learn that this field had been the scene of the main battle for Clane in 1798. It was also the location where my father was to uncover a large double-edged curved sword when ploughing a few years later.

School holidays came a month or so early for us that summer as my brother and I were helping my father to do renovations on the old house. The house had originally been a long thatched one with a single storey. Electricity had come early to Clane when a line was brought to Clongowes, and the then-owner of our house, Johnny Kenny, had got some old second-hand timber from Clongowes and raised two thirds of the house to two storeys, leaving the remainder as a shed. In 1973 my father and I converted this shed into Clane's first library.

Kenny's daughter had married a Wexford man named Kearns and they were then moving to that part of the country, so they were selling the house. On moving to Clane we became the owners of about three acres, which they had behind the house, and twelve acres in Blackhall. For many years we rented a field beside the house and another on the Dublin road from Billy Reddy, who along with his sister, owned and ran a shop at the two-storey thatched house that preceded Blake's VG, later O'Cléirigh's and now Londis. We kept three cows and a horse to draw a cart, with which, with neighbours, we ploughed and tilled when the season came. We raised our own calves and bought in others. We fattened up to six pigs at a time. The cattle, we generally drove to the fair in Naas, while the pigs were sent to the Dublin market. Kit Walsh and Billy Graham were lorry men who collected pigs before daybreak for this purpose. This was still the era of self-sufficiency. Like everyone else, we grew all our own potatoes and vegetables, made our own butter, cured our own bacon, had hens, chickens, ducks and turkeys, apples, gooseberries, blackcurrants, raspberries, and cut our own turf. Everyone kept a vegetable garden in those days. In the summer my father would take meadows at auction. As tractors became more common in the fifties, we rented an increasing acreage for grain crops, working through tillage contractors. All members of the family had their jobs to do, both boys and girls, in addition to schoolwork. There were seven of us in the family, two boys and five girls.

There were two teachers in the boys' school where the KARE Centre and tennis club are now located on the Dublin road. These were Dr Holland and Mrs Holland, his wife. Dr Holland taught third, fourth, fifth and sixth classes in one room, while Mrs Holland taught High Infants, First and Second Classes in the other room. Boys traditionally went to the convent school for the Junior Infant year. The doctor and Mrs Holland lived in the Teachers' House, which is the two-storey house just beyond the school, where Lynchs now live. The master was unique in all of Ireland, though we probably did not realise it at the time. His qualifications outmatched all the inspectors and staff of the Department of Education. He was from Cork but when he and his wife retired they moved to Waterford. When he died, his obituary revealed that he had an M.A., Ph.D. and D.Litt. I remember him more for his sense of humour and some of the stories he told than anything else. The inspectors were said to be shy of him and rarely came near the place. He had two small eccentricities, which would not be tolerated nowadays: he smoked in class – using a long cigarette holder – and he allowed his dog into class to sleep by the fire. There were about sixty in all in the boys' school in those days, and a similar number in the girls' school. The population of Clane was around 300. Very few went on to secondary school, as this involved cycling to Naas to the Christian Brothers or to the Mercy Convent. There were in fact only two day secondary schools for boys in the whole county – Naas and Athy. Around that time the first few vocational schools had just opened, including Prosperous. There was almost an assumption that you would be finishing your schooling at the age of fourteen.

Going back to the first primary schools, prior to the middle of the nineteenth century, the teachers have come almost exclusively from the South or West coast and they had an educational theory known as the 'Bullock Theory' in relation to Kildare and a few other Leinster counties. The theory was that we lacked motivation and were difficult to teach and that this was because the land was so good and the cattle fattened so easily. Our future was secure and we did not see the need for education. I remember occasionally the master would come back after lunch and approach an imaginary four-bar gate at the front of the room on which he would place his elbows and survey the assembled classes. 'I think I will put a few of you out on new grass', he would say, 'McEvoy and whoever move up here to the front'. It was years later that I heard of the 'Bullock Theory'. The theory is flawed it would appear. Whether secondary schools were set up or not depended on the bishop issuing an invitation to an order to do so. In contrast with many other parts of the country, formal primary education existed in the parishes of Kildare decades before it was taken over by the State in 1839. The bishops, having done a good job in this regard, sat back on their laurels while other parts of the country, which came much later into primary education, used the newly-found momentum to follow up with the creation of secondary facilities more or less following on directly.

The school vegetable garden was an institution under Dr Holland. In those days the school building was only about half its present length and the vegetable garden ran by the road frontage from the near end of the school down to the hedge that presently forms the boundary with Central Park. There was a dry toilet over the deep ditch at this point, just inside the roadside wall. In those days the wall was not interrupted by the present entrance to the tennis club. The junior classes played just behind the school building and the older boys had goal posts set up in the back where the tennis courts are now. The master brought his classes out to work in the vegetable garden for about two hours in the week. It was good exercise and a welcome break that we looked forward to. Every type of vegetable was grown. The produce was largely consumed by the master and Mrs Holland, though he often bestowed bags of rhubarb, radishes, scallions, lettuce or whatever on deserving cases.

The summers of our past always seem long and filled with sunshine. The days were long and filled with jobs to be done. Apart from the daily routine of milking cows and feeding calves there was hay to be made and brought home. Neighbours who helped us also had to be helped in due course. The job I disliked most was spending all day on my knees weeding drills of potatoes or thinning turnips. There were no weed killers in those days. We usually cut our turf on the Downings Bog in Prosperous where we rented a turf bank. We owned our own patch on the Kilmurry Bog but the quality was not as good. In good weather we liked to swim in the Liffey just above the weir. This was a popular activity on Sunday afternoons or on warm summer evenings after a day's work. Another popular venue were the Liffey banks at Hickey's, across the fields from where Curran and Ganly are now located on the Dublin road. Other popular pastimes of the day were hunting for rabbits with terriers and fishing in the canal. Boys did not hang around in groups as is popular nowadays, but met in twos and threes to hunt or fish. The only times groups gathered was to play pitch and toss or to talk together outside the church after Mass. The popular venues for pitch and toss were in front of Reddy's forge, which faced the road from what is now the paved area of the Stream Park at the entrance to the Millicent road, and Firmount Cross. There was an unspoken consensus that pitch and toss was a socially unacceptable form of gambling and the gardaí had the authority to break up such schools and move them on. Sundays after Mass and in the afternoon were the popular occasion for such challenges, when farm workers, dressed in their Sunday best, enjoyed a few hours of freedom. Other forms of entertainment were of course football and camogie. The GAA enjoyed the use of a field belonging to Manzor's which was at the outer end of what is now Loughbollard Estate. Following the local county teams was always a popular pursuit in Clane from 1884.

The Loughbollard field: Manzor's 'football field', with Kelly's bread van on the road.

Clane hall, the old corrugated iron-roofed building on the College Road, was built in 1925 because of a local interest in amateur dramatics inspired by Father Fannon CC As a result of a concert held in Slevin's Mill, which stood on the Naas side of the Liffey Bridge and has long been demolished, £12 were raised and the site of a shed was bought from Johnny Kenny for £15. The hall eventually came into the possession of the GAA and they built an extension to it around 1950. They passed it on in due course to the Youth Club. Dances were held in the hall every Saturday night throughout the fifties and before. Up to 100 bicycles would be parked in our yard beside the hall. Pictures were shown in the hall every Thursday night by a Mr Price from Prosperous, who also ran a cinema in his own village. The most popular films were cowboys, serials and *Laurel and Hardy*. There was always a great air of excitement when a travelling show came to the hall for a week or a carnival came to the football field. They were happy times really. Card games and visiting for a chat were popular in the majority of houses around Clane in those years before television. Racing and the placing of bets was always popular and Punchestown brought everything to a standstill.

There were four pubs in Clane in those days: Manzor's, Jones', Carroll's and O'Neill's. Carroll's was at the site of what is now Corner House, and had previously been Geoghegan's for generations. Bernard Carroll was a retired primary teacher from Strokestown. The publican background was on his wife's side of the family. She had a brother who was a Jesuit, Father O'Beirne, who taught Latin and Greek in Clongowes. Mrs Jones, a widow, ran the present Fagan's with the help of her brother, Joe Whelan. In previous generations the pub was known as Whelan's. O'Neill's was located where the Peony Palace and Video Shop now stand. It had been operating under that name from the second half of the previous century but had closed down, I believe, some time before our arrival in Clane. Manzor's and Jones' operated small family groceries in conjunction with their licensed trade. Apart from these two there were grocery shops at Lavin's, where Spar is now located and McKenna's. Lavin's had only opened shortly before our arrival in Clane, while McKenna's opened that same year, 1948. The grocery trade was rather simple as people were largely self-sufficient. Bakers' bread, largely Kelly's of Kilcock, Cunningham of Naas and Boland's, was delivered regularly but there was also a big trade in loose flour, as people baked a lot of their own. A problem with the pub grocery was that the unwrapped bread tended to take on the flavour of cigarette smoke. We had no regular bank in Clane until the early seventies. The Ulster Bank used to visit Jones' once a week and customers entered the back parlour privately to do their business, like going to confession.

The roads were quiet and safe to walk or cycle on in those days. The only time you would see any significant number of cars was when Punchestown came around. The children had the custom of waving to them as they passed, which probably went back to a tradition of paying respect to the gentry as they passed in their carriages. People kept notebooks and counted the cars as they passed. Incredible numbers, like 100-plus for the day, never failed to raise eyebrows.

The horse and cart remained the dominant form of transport until the early sixties. When eventually the Main Street filled with parked cars in the seventies it only did so for 11.30a. m. Mass on Sundays. It was safe to let your teenage children off to school on their bicycles to Naas or Prosperous. This was before free education, which was introduced around 1967. The Christian Brothers were very reasonable with their fees, charging only £3 per term, and as a second boy from the same family I was accepted free. Everything was done to keep costs down, including the recycling of second-hand books. A Brother gave up part of his own lunchtime to make pots of tea for the boys from the country. During the Inter Cert and Leaving those boys from the country were sent to the Five Lamps restaurant for a full lunch paid for by the Brothers. In my time there were about a dozen boys cycling from Clane. There was an almost equal number of girls cycling to the convent. There was very little contact between boys and girls along the road. Cows had to be milked and fed and put out to grass before leaving for school at 8.30a.m. so we would arrive at 9.00a.m. each morning, Saturdays included.

You had to get used to hardship and frequently getting wet. The teachers were very strict on time and on having all the homework done, which could take between three and four hours each night. You had to pass your summer test each year or repeat the year. Faced with this choice there was an occasional drop-out. We had a half-day for football and sports on a Wednesday afternoon. This was much looked-forward-to. This was the routine of our lives and the wind was nearly always in our faces. The holidays were always welcome, especially the three months of June, July and August. If you were hoping to go on to college you could earn some money in the summer, footing turf with Bórd na Móna. You might invest this in a few calves or pigs. The fee to study science in UCD was only £70 per year and a bit less for Arts. A good neighbour could provide a lift to Dublin each morning. You could get a week's travel home on the bus for £1.

A number of things stick out in my memories of those years. A high wind brought a giant tree crashing down just in front of a group of us as we cycled home around the bend at the gates of Castlesize at the Bodenstown junction one day. It crunched through the concrete wall of a cowshed that runs by the road's edge on the far side. The leaders were slapped by the finer tips of the branches.

On another occasion an unbelievably strong gust of wind came from my left through the little walled entrance which up until a few years ago formed the junction to the Moat Commons Lane and lifted me clean off the ground, bike, bag and all, with the wheels and pedals spinning. I was dropped on the far side of the road and continued on my way.

The most horrific weather conditions of the century occurred on 8 December 1954, when a hurricane was centred over Kildare and Wicklow. Nineteen centimetres (or eight inches) of rain fell in one day. Flooding was so severe that the ESB lost control of the dam at Poulaphouca. There was huge flooding downstream at several locations with almost a square mile going under water at Clane. In places this flooding was up to ten feet deep. The eyes of the Liffey Bridge were almost closed off and the Council was afraid it would be pushed. The Naas road was cut off with the water coming as far as the Corner House and through the gardens on both sides of the Main Street. From roughly Behan's garage outwards the water crossed through culverts under the Dublin road and back to the edge of the Capdoo Lane. This had been the old road to Dublin up until 1780. It remained just above flood level. The Dublin road had been built by the engineer Mosse to just exceed the flood level. This it did, with the water up to both edges and extending beyond the normal course of the river into Rathmore, Blackhall. The water came to the top of the steps of the cottages leading around the bend to Abbeylands and inundated the gardens and low fields behind. The old people at the time remembered comparable floods before the building of the Poulaphouca dam and they had become lulled into the false belief that this was now a thing of the past.

XIX

FROM A NEEDLE TO AN ANCHOR

Tony McKenna

Picture this if you can. The year is 1948. The Second World War is over and a new era is on the horizon. Thoughts of getting married and establishing a business are a major challenge. These momentous events were on the minds of John McKenna and his soon-to-be bride Brigid Morrin. Both had worked in Cunningham's of Naas, a business icon in its own right, and had decided to marry and start a grocery and provisions business in Clane. Thus in September 1948 the business that bears his name was established.

As anyone can imagine, supplies of the most basic grocery needs were very restricted and at times non-existent. This, however, did not deter John and Brigid McKenna. Having many contacts with the wholesalers was a major coup and thus the slogan 'When in need and in despair – just come to McKenna's you'll get it there' was invented. The business flourished and gradually other lines were added, such as light hardware, giftware, drapery and farm supplies. Things progressed as most things do, until April 1967 when tragedy struck – John, at the early age of fifty-four, died suddenly, leaving his wife, Brigid, to run the business and provide for their two school-going sons, Tony and Seán.

This she did with admirable courage, overcoming many difficulties. Tony was to join the business in the late sixties followed some years later by Seán. The business flourished and moved more into the hardware trade, catering to the ever-increasing needs of the expanding Clane area. However, more tragedy was to hit the business when in June 1981 Brigid died, following a long illness.

Once again the business had to re-invent itself. More and more the business went in the DIY and hardware direction. So, in 1986 the current premises opened to widespread acclaim. It was one of the first purpose-built hardware and DIY stores built in County Kildare, and it attracts customers from far and wide. The business boasts the widest selection with expert advice – two ingredients sadly lacking in many of today's businesses. Here's to the future – with the next phase seeing this family-owned business move boldly forward to meet the needs of the twenty-first century.

John and Brigid McKenna with their son Tony.

J.P. McKenna's old shop.

XX

AD DEUM QUI LAETIFICAT

Bryan Sammon

It was quite usual every so often for Father Doyle, parish priest, as manager of the National School to come in and talk to the teachers and find out how things were going in general. But when we saw Father Hughes, the curate, with the newly-appointed curate Father Kehoe, who had just been ordained in Rome, coming into the school, we sensed something different was going to happen. And so it did. Both Father Hughes and Father Kehoe were in on a mission – the mission to select altar boys – the new group. The qualifications were to live in fairly close proximity to the parish church – or at least to be able to cycle in and be on time for the various Masses and ceremonies – and, of course, the other big test was to be able to answer the responses at Mass in Latin.

Initially, the senior boy would tutor us in Latin and then a month later, both priests came in and examined us in our proficiency at pronunciation in Latin. It has to be said that there was many a stumble over some of the words and we even detected a smile on the faces of both priests. While one would be able to give most of the responses, it was the 'De Profundis' said at funerals that claimed the most victims, and indeed claimed victims right up to the age of fifteen and upwards. The words in the 'De Profundis' were very long, hard, and difficult. Nobody was ever turned away and so the new group of altar boys came in 1956, and donned the red soutane and the white starched surplices.

The older boys of course, during Mass, did all the actions, movements and duties required. We just knelt and observed. The duties were serving 'right', 'left' and the bell. It became practice that the person who arrived first at the church got the preference in serving 'right', 'left' or the bell with the result that for 11.00a.m. Mass on a Sunday, altar boys would be seen going in at 10a.m. to be able to say 'I was in' and claim their case in the three major duties. It must be remembered that all our memories of serving at Mass were in the pre-1964 or pre-Vatican II era, so the priest had his back to the people all the time except when he came down the church and went into the pulpit where he gave a sermon. We remember that during Mass there would be fits of coughing. In fact, coughing started when Mass began, but when it came to the sermon the coughing was suppressed, and when the priest had finished the sermon the suppressed silence gave way to more bouts of coughing.

Early after Christmas, Easter and in October, the dues were read from the pulpit. This was where each townland was read out at Sunday Masses at 8.00a.m. and 11.00a.m., with all donors ranked according to contribution from the top, which was £5, to the lowest, which was 2s. We had Benediction with the Blessing of the Blessed Sacrament with the thurible, and the incense

Interior of St Patrick and Brigid's church, Clane.

and singing of 'Osalutaris Hostia', 'Tantum Ergo' and at the very end, 'Hail Queen of Heaven' and 'We Stand for God', backbone of which were Seán Cullen and Des Marron.

The highlight of the church year were the Easter ceremonies, starting on Holy Thursday evening and winding up on Easter Sunday. Having Father Kehoe as curate and having just come from Rome, we altar boys were given the highest training in the ceremonies. The Sunday after Easter Sunday we had the forty hours in which the Blessed Sacrament, after High Mass, was exposed until Monday morning, and there was a roster of volunteers so the church would never be vacant, even at 3.00a.m. in the morning. Generally, in late May we had the feast of Corpus Christi which, on the Thursday, brought the village to a stand-still because everyone participated in the procession. All around the village the rosary was recited, hymns were sung and Benediction took place in Dalton's house, which is now Dr Flanagan's residence.

Mother Joseph was truly a remarkable person and indeed some would say she deserves sainthood. She was for a time Reverend Mother. She also taught in the school, was the organist and helped in the sacristy to make sure that everything was alright. She was literally everywhere. She used to recount to us various stories about Father John Sullivan SJ, who was on the staff of Clongowes Wood College. One day, as he was being brought in the main door, he enquired of the Sister how everyone was in the community. 'All are very well, thank God, Father'. He said 'You should never say that once there is a person sick among you, it always brings great blessings.' Also, Father John is supposed to have foretold that there would never be a fatal accident at Manzor's corner – long may that prediction continue to hold true. Along with all other duties and responsibilities, Mother Joseph was always among the flowers, preparing them in the vases to put on the altar. She advocated putting pennies with daffodils and Aspro tablets with tulips, as it prolonged their lives! A truly remarkable person. She also told us that Dom Marmion often played in the Main Street – little did we know that this man would be beatified in the twenty-first century.

A man for all seasons: Father
Patrick Kehoe CC, 1960.

The sacristan, Paddy McCormack, was so reliable that it was said he was never late in opening up the gates in the morning time except on one occasion, on the Monday morning after the Sunday on which Clane won the Senior County championship in 1963. Besides all the mundane activities and duties, Paddy rang the bell for all Masses and also allowed us altar boys to help him in the counting of the collection; and there we saw the pennies, the three-penny pieces, the six penny bits and on occasion, the shillings. A highlight for us was to help Paddy bring the life-sized figures for the crib from the vault of the church. It was quite a task and challenge, as three boys were needed per statue and we had to negotiate six steps up into the church, but the mission was always accomplished.

Confirmation came every three years, and those in fourth, fifth and sixth class at the time were presented to the bishop. If one was serving, one had the honour of either holding the bishop's mitre or crozier during the ceremony. The bishop would go around the various pews asking questions on religious knowledge and it is said that nobody ever failed to answer, a credit to the primary teachers who had everybody up to such a high standard.

Every three years was the Mission. The Mission was very special. It was given by three priests from a religious order – Augustinians, Jesuits, Passionist – but it is the Redemptorists who stuck in our minds. Generally, there were three priests: one could be considered very nice, another person was 'middle of the road' and then there was always the hard priest who literally thumped the pulpit in his half an hour to three quarters-of-an-hour sermon each evening.

Every evening, there was a long line for confession and sometimes the dialogue could be heard in the pews outside; some were red-faced. Outside, on the Main Street, were mobile huts set up by visiting traders for the duration of the Mission. Rosary beads, medals, prayer books, statues and many other objects of piety were available. All objects were blessed on the last night of the Mission.

Father John Doyle PP keeps
a watchful eye.

There were also other devotions which we altar boys had to attend to. There were the May
Devotions, the October Devotions whereby on every Wednesday and Friday, there was rosary
and Benediction, and of course during the month of Lent there were the Stations of the Cross,
the Holy Hour, which was the first Friday of every month, and the Sodality, which was the
first Sunday of every month, so being an altar boy was a very busy position.

Funerals came into the church and were the same as they are now, except that the coffin was
placed in the back left-hand side surrounded by four beeswax candles lit while the church was
open, and around the same place was the baptismal font, so in the same area we had babies brought
and on sad occasions, the funerals. Another ceremony that was rather mysterious to us altar boys
was that of churching: on a Sunday we would tell the priest that there was a woman over at Our
Lady's Altar waiting to be churched. At the time we did not know or participate in the ceremony,
but we later learned that this was a medieval ceremony that took place after childbirth in which
the mother came in thanksgiving, to be cleansed and to be given the grace to rear the baby.

The parish boundaries prior to 1972 extended to Staplestown, Timahoe, Coill Dubh and
Rathcoffey and this very large area was served by the parish priest and two curates. The
convent school was allowed to take boys for two years in Infants, in preparation for their First
Holy Communion, and it was always considered a plus to make your First Holy Communion
with the nuns – as opposed to making it in the boys' school – because of the great party they
had afterwards. This was in the 1950s.

The Church of Ireland church of St Michael's in Millicent was always a somewhat
mysterious place, and not a place to visit. You have to remember that we were in the era just
after the Taoiseach and government ministers having stood outside St Patrick's Cathedral at the
funeral of the former President, Dr Douglas Hyde. We befriended a boy, Ronnie Hempenstall,
who lived with his mother and father opposite the church and to our great surprise, he was
just like anyone of us, came on the hunts, laughed and participated in all our games. On one
occasion, the wife of Archdeacon Handy saw the group of us and brought us in on a tour of
the beautiful church and one thing she said to us that has lasted the test of time, was, 'It's like
as if we are all in different boats sailing, but we are all going to the same destination'. And so
'to the God who gives us joy', which is the translation of the title of this chapter.

LIST OF PARISH PRIESTS (1731 – 2006)

Clane – Staplestown area

Father Kedagh Molloy (--1731--)

Clane, Staplestown and Rathcoffey united as one parish.

Father Andrew Ennis PP (--1738--)

The name of the Parish Priest from this period may be missing

Father William Dunne PP (----- 1793)

Father John Dunne PP (1793-1797)

Father John Lalor PP (1797-1803)

Father John Robinson PP (1802-1810)

Father Mark Kennedy PP (1810-1821)

Father Malachy McMahon PP (1821-1824)

Father Maurice Kearney PP (1824-1842)

Father Edward Conroy PP (1842-1872)

Father Patrick Turner PP (1872-1889)

Father James Colgan PP (1889-1926)

Father Laurence Keogh PP (1926-1948)

Father John Doyle PP (1948-1972)

Clane/Rathcoffey Parish

Father William Hughes PP (1972-1981)

Father Richard Kelly PP (1981-1995)

Father Denis Harrington PP (1995- ----)

CURATES WHO SERVED IN CLANE PARISH (1900-2006)

Father John Fenton CC

Father John Foley CC

Father Michael Byrne CC

Father William Rice CC

Father M. Conroy CC

Father P. O'Haire CC

Father M.C. Kelly CC

Father L. O'Fionnain CC

Father P.G. Walsh CC

Father T.P. Murphy CC

Father Thomas Gahan CC

Father M Hayes CC

Father J.W. McDonnell CC

Father E. Curran CC

Father Michael Gleeson CC

Father John Mooney CC

Father Jack O'Leary CC

FatherWillie Hughes CC

Father Patrick Kehoe CC

Father John Gahan CC

Father T. Coonan CC

Father Brendan Byrne CC

Father Cathal Cullen CC

Father Tommy O'Malley CC

Father Bernard Jordan CC

Father P. McDonald CC

Father Ed Flood CC

Father J. Dalton CC

Father Richard Hogan CC

Father Bob Thompson SJ

Father Patrick Hennessy CC

Father Willie O'Byrne CC

Father Paul Dempsey CC

Father Paul O'Boyle C C

Bryan Sammon leads procession in convent gardens, with Breda Keary.

THOSE WHO SERVED CLANE AND DONADEA PARISH FROM 1883

Millicent Church built 1883; Donadea parish joined to Clane in 1924

1862 – Ambrose Cooke

1888 – William Sherlock

1913 – Herbert N. Graigue

1929 – Percy Coster

1934 – Brian Handy

1974 – Paul Cardew

1979 – Frederick Gilmore

1984 – Adrian Empey

1988 – David Frazer

2006 –Kevin Rohnnè

Back row: Billy Geraghty, Pat Ryan, Lar Higgins, John Nevin. Front row: David Mahony, Peter McIntyre, Noel Nevin.'

The old Parochial House.

Gerry Walsh on his Communion Day, with sisters Brendan, Anna and Joseph.

Staplestown Church.

XXI

SNAPSHOTS OF CHILDHOOD

Bryan Sammon

All of us have memories of primary school. My initial memory in Infants was the chart on the wall showing various animals with a name in Irish beneath them. It was such an achievement for a five-year-old to know the meaning of *bó*, *capall* and *cearc*. It was essential for everyone to learn the phrase '*An bhfuil cead agam dul amach*' as this was your passport to get permission from the teacher to go to the toilet. The visit to the toilet was sometimes not the mission but a three or four-minute private break from the daily timetable of the school day. We then learned about adding simple figures and then progressed to subtraction, or what we termed 'take-away' sums. The day passed quite quickly as it was divided up into different activities: Irish spelling, English reading, and the large map of Ireland, which was studied in great detail. Christian Doctrine was always at mid-day and we knew then that lunch-time was only thirty minutes away.

Every fortnight, our teacher Mrs Armstrong encouraged sixty boys between five-and nine to participate in forty-five minutes of singing. *Trasna na Dtonnta* and *O Ró mo Bhaidn* were tackled with great gusto, as it was a relief from the hectic work of headline writing with a special pen and nib, every so often dipped into the ink-well in the middle of the desk. Biros were unheard of or if they were available, they were strictly forbidden. Mrs Armstrong played a most important part of our young lives, as she was the person who first brought us to deal with sums, Irish, English reading, writing and singing – a truly versatile teacher, dealing with five to nine-year-olds.

Every year or so, the dentist visited the school and earned for himself the title 'the Butcher'. As far as I can remember, fillings were unheard of and extractions were the order of the day. We often felt that the dentist was being paid a fee for each extraction rather than his day's visit to the school. Looking back now, the procedure was very primitive. Desks were pulled together with newspaper on top of four of them, with a receptacle on the floor to receive the teeth. After the extraction, the unfortunate boy was allowed out into the school grounds for fresh air and the spitting of blood. Again, this turned into a competition to see how much blood was spat out on the ground by each victim. There was the odd example of some unfortunate boy having a dizzy spell or fainting. Thankfully, this is no longer so and young people look forward to their visit to the dentist.

Playtime could become rather robust at times with some unfortunate student getting his ears rubbed behind the lunch shed. We played football, but with forty students participating! Stamp collecting was always very popular and Stephen Curran took pride in having the biggest and most valuable collection in the school. He never brought his collection in, but on being challenged, he did so on one particular day. During lunch-time, we all clustered around

Above left: Three good men: Thomas Sammon, Dick Coffey, and Bryan Sammon.

Above right: Mrs Armstrong, teacher.

Left: Bryan Sammon and Lassie: a cowboy and his dog.

Stephen like a swarm of bees to try and gain a glimpse of this treasure. Unfortunately (for Stephen), some overzealous boy took a particular fancy to a triangular stamp from Bermuda with a white swan on it – it got torn and Stephen got most upset and that was the end of public exhibitions of his stamp album.

School finished at 3.00p.m. and so started the next part of our lives. McKenna's shop was the nearest to the school and was obviously well-frequented. Mr McKenna had, above all items in his

Billy Noble (Jones' Bar).

Josie Doyle and Carmel Marron.

LDF in the early Forties, Clongowes Wood College.

shop, a blackboard that advertised various special items he had a bargain for each week. Inevitably, some of the prices were rubbed out with small pieces of chalk taken from the school and used to highly inflate the cost of rashers, oranges or flour. This certainly did not boost trade for Mr McKenna! Also, every Sunday whenever a GAA match was being played in Croke Park, Mr McKenna would have the teams written up on the same blackboard, waiting for the results to be filled in. Again, unfortunately, there was always somebody to fill in the wrong results for him.

The year sped by very quickly, as there were always simple pastimes to be enjoyed. Marbles, hopscotch, and at Halloween, collecting chestnuts and having competitions to find out who had the best conker. Then the time of year came when a group of us with all the dogs of every breed we could collect went on a 'hunt'. I remember Liam's father expressing surprise and amazement and saying 'You are not taking my lovely dog Trixie with you, are you?', to which Liam and Pat answered 'We are Dad'. So much for the fourth commandment! Dick Coffey was generous enough to allow us to walk across his land, as there was always livestock grazing there. Our aim was to catch rabbits, but even if we saw one rabbit in the afternoon, it was considered to be a good day's work.

August and September were the mushroom months. We headed off on the 'rampart' (the short cut to Clongowes Wood College) to go into the large Brick field. In our innocence we didn't realise that we were walking on a very historical border, which the government in Dublin Castle had decided to build in the form of a double ditch from Dundalk to Trim to Kilcock, Clane, Naas and on to Dalkey, in 1494. In this field, no matter how large the group was, we always succeeded in getting a hank of mushrooms, if not a small canful. How delicious those mushrooms were, fried in butter and with plenty of salt, eaten with brown bread and butter for tea. Not the healthiest combination according to today's medical teachings.

We tried fishing in the small rivers, but pinkeens were our catch. It was Mr McManmon and his sons Paddy and Seán who caught the salmon, trout and even pike in the Liffey. Wonderful fishermen they all were. Seán always told us that if we were patient enough, eels could be caught in the Gollymochy River – we never succeeded.

'I'll see to that roof tomorrow.' – Garret O'Rourke.

Tillie Behan.

During the summer, a carnival took place in Rathcoffey. We were on our bikes at 7.00p.m. and home by 11.00p. m. In those four hours, we had enjoyment all the way. Besides the usual amusements, there was always the roulette, which Ned O'Neill was in charge of. Having made 'big profits' from the adults, Ned was very generous to us children. As he swung the turntable around, he always ensured by discretely putting his hand under the table, that it clicked into the right niche, to pay out as many pennies as possible to our eager faces. Having thanked him and being able now to purchase a 4d. and indeed sometimes, a 6d. ice-cream, we could now watch the great seven-a-side football matches. As well as local teams, UCD, the Air Corps and some Meath teams took part. The prizes for the winners were either a set of wrist watches or enough material to make a gentleman's suit.

Every day during the summer was a sunny day, full blue sky – it never rained! This gave us the daily opportunity to go down to the Liffey to paddle and later swim. Bill Hickey was very kind, as the group of us had to pass by his house and enter his lands to get there. It was the first time that we saw Bantam hens and Paddy Donnelly assured us that their eggs were just as big as those of the bigger hens – we weren't sure if this was true or false. Trips to the Liffey often occurred three times a day, with sandwiches, chocolate, and the transistor. Would you blame us when you had two damsels like Carmel and Josie to look at?

On our way down through Clane, we might meet Joe Bibby, who would put his hands up to his eyes, pretending he was looking through binoculars and giving a commentary on an imaginary horse race. Garret O'Rourke was always on the roadside, smoking his pipe and wishing us well, waiting for his niece Emily to bring home the cow that was grazing on the verges of the approach roads to Clane. Billy Noble, who worked for O'Neill's, would sometimes say, 'well lads, was the water wet today', to which we would retort, 'No Billy, it's still very dry! Jimmy Anderson would attempt to give us a demonstration on the roadside of the proper way to swim. He would say 'Keep your head above the water lads and keep your arms going like this'. He was in fact demonstrating the 'dog's paddle'. Pat Quinn, who worked for John McEvoy, a generous man, made Paddy his favourite, as he would buy him a cone on many occasions.

Now and then, we saw Mrs Leddy and her bag, walking quickly, on some mission. Paddy and Liam, in hushed tones, would tell us what she was about in their language. Mrs Leddy was the local mid-wife. Dr Michael Walsh was very dedicated to all aspects of health. He was on call twenty-four hours a day, and with his nearest colleague, Dr Michael Purcell, he looked after a very wide geographical area. Dr Walsh himself tells the story that one day at about 10.00a.m. in the morning, he received two phone calls from a lady who lived in a certain area in Timahoe. Being the dedicated doctor he was, he suspended all immediate duties and drove to the lady. He was uncertain of where precisely the lady lived and arriving there, he met a woman carrying two heavy buckets of water. He enquired of her where Mrs --- lived and she

Above: Turning the hay, Billy Harrington.

Left: Thirsty work! Paddy Walsh, Digby Bridge.

immediately replied 'Ah! Is it yourself doctor, how are you? I am the woman who rang you an hour ago. Come on in and I will give you a cup of tea – you must be tired!' On retelling the story, Dr Walsh always ended with his customary hearty laugh.

August was a busy month because it also was the haymaking season, with the cocking of the hay and sitting down to well-earned refreshments, Peter Rourke and Phil Purcell would entertain us with endless stories, most of them fictional. They both were magicians, as they could make frogs appear and disappear as often as they wished. The turning of hay, the cocking of hay and the 'topping' of the cocks of hay and finally, the cocks of hay being pulled up on the bogey and us getting lifts at the back – all of that came to an end when the baler trundled into the village with Paddy and Seamus Doherty. Later we stood in awe as they brought the Massive John Deere combine harvester through the village. We knew then that the threshing days were over for good.

Pat O'Connor, of Clane community school, marries Mary O'Connor.

When car registrations started with 10. Bryan and Lassie.

In 1961 we witnessed the arrival of a visionary and inspirational figure in the person of Sister Perpetua. Uplifting morale, she began, along with Sister Lucy, to set up second-level education for the area in the form of the Secondary Top. In 1967, with the beginning of free education, Sister Perpetua and Sister Lucy, along with their fellow Sisters, made the momentous decision not only to enter the new scheme, but also to allow boys come into first year. On a personal note, this made my appointment to the staff possible. Secondary education, with the Sisters and lay staff, Kathleen Quille, Mary O'Farrell, Maura Anglim, Christy McQuinn, Tony McEvoy, Pat O'Connor, Maura Weedle, Kathleen Heneghan, Mary Donohue along with John Kearney, Pat Kilfeather, Janice Leytham and Elizabeth Higgins, a former student, laid the foundations of what is now Scoil Mhuire Community School, with 750 day students and even more night students, and a staff of sixty.

Father Brian Cullen SJ founded the Society for the Relief of the Poor and Aged. This association provided wonderful help in every way through the students of the college to a number of families in the area who required it. For Father Cullen the problem arose as to how this service was to be continued over the summer months. Liam, Paddy and I volunteered and so on the first Saturday in June, we set off in Paddy's uncle Edmund's mini-bus, which he very generously entrusted to his nephew every week and with ten wholesome hampers purchased in John Blake's supermarket, we set out to the various families in the area. We received a great welcome from one and all, as they had been doubtful as to what would happen during the summer. Besides the weekly hamper, it was the chat and human contact that many of these people required, and we were delighted to provide that for them.

In 1969, an inter-village talent competition was organised by a special committee in Maynooth and all contests were held there. In the first year Clane did not get far, but the following year events unfolded differently. On the quiz team were Pat Lynch, Pat O'Connor, Pat Behan and Tony McEvoy. How could any team conquer them? In the talent competition, each village had to put forward eight different acts. We put forward the following:

Irish Dancing - Peg Nugent, Anne Blake and Kathleen Behan

Rajah – The Eastern Magician - the one and only Michael Weedle

Harpist - Kathleen Dorsch

'Here's Pat' - the versatile Pat Behan (Father of Paddy). This act was based on the TV series *Here's Harry* featuring Harry Worth, which was very popular at the time. This involved Pat going out on his own and telling stories and jokes for up to seven minutes – a daunting task, but not to our Pat

'Two Little Boys' - Victor Marron and Robert Kelly, on their rocking horse, singing Rolf Harris's popular song at the time

Des Marron singing 'The Road to Mandalay' and 'Goodbye' made famous by Joseph Locke

The Toff and the Tramp - Liam and myself

The Story of Ireland - 1916 to 1922. This was a Pageant of about fifteen minutes' duration, featuring Sally McCormack, Elizabeth Higgins, Rita McCormack, Des Marron, Liam and myself as narrator.

After two wins, we reached the semi-final and won, and were then pitted against Dunboyne, who had great experience in county Meath competitions. But on the night, the three adjudicators declared Clane the winners for 1970. I am sure no one will disagree when you read through the line-up of talent.

The approach roads to Clane were kept spotlessly clean and not a single weed could be seen from March to October. This was due to the hard work and perseverance of Dinny Peggs and Patsy Gorman, both of whom were employed by the County Council. They were succeeded by Jack Graham, who felt it was unfair that this burden should be placed on the shoulders of one person – so he mixed hard work with social life. Jack would hold conversations along the road with any person who wished to know about the latest death, a run-down of the match of last Sunday, or the gory details of some melee that took place in the surrounding district. While we knew all of the above characters, there are two worth mentioning who were dead before we came to the use of reason.

At the end of the village (Naas end) was an establishment run by Ms Aggie Weir, who had a welcome for everybody, particularly men who had been walking long distances (Knights of

Above: A cycle race starts at the Corner House, Clane.

Right: Mary Connolly, Tom Behan, Olive Connolly.

the Road) or maybe had obtained part-time agricultural work and needed lodgings. Tradition has it that the comforts were very basic. There were some beds with mattresses but sleeping on the floor would also be allowed. If a person wanted the comfort of turning during sleep, a penny was the fee. However, if one could lie straight for the night, a halfpenny was the cost. Meals were extra, and during the day Aggie, who always wore black, could be seen coming from Geoghegan's butcher stall with a good amount of pigs' bladders, which would be on the daily menu. I do not think that à la carte was a possibility at Aggie's.

Another character was 'Butcher' Gahon, who lived in the Mainham–Betaghstown area. Every Sunday, he would walk to Mass in Rathcoffey. On a particular Sunday, Father Keogh PP got a puncture at Boherhole Cross. After greeting Father Keogh, Butcher continued walking towards Rathcoffey. 'Are you not going to help me with the wheel, butcher'? 'Oh, I couldn't do that Father; I would be late for Mass!' Such were the colourful characters of that era.

Our childhood years were also enhanced by hearing of the great cycling achievements of Mick Doherty on the special circuit track around Croke Park. It was generally agreed that Mick was of Olympic standard and would have made the Olympic team for Ireland in 1940 but unfortunately, due to the Second World War, no games were held. Cycling was always a feature in the life of the village due mainly to the efforts of Patsy Farrell who always encouraged young people to join the local club. There was always good fun and sport and two characters who were extremely funny were Tom Behan and Jackie Geoghegan – they were adults but entered into our games on occasions. It was only later in life that we realised that Tom and Jackie were God's own children and are now surely in Heaven.

Voting Day always brought extra excitement to the village. Paddy Woods – 'the Volkswagen King of Leinster', a most jovial man, was always the last person to vote and could be seen emerging from the boys' school at two minutes to nine. Members of the gardaí were always looked upon as friends and were always held in the highest esteem. We were told of the terrible deed in 1948, when part of St Michael's Church in Millicent was destroyed by fire. But due to the wonderful investigating team of Sergeant Marron, Gardaí Lee, Ahern, O'Donnell and McGuinness, the person responsible was brought to court and punished. Later on when Clane Youth Club was founded, Sergeant Bill Egan and Garda Martin Gleeson were truly friends and always looked in to the hall to see how things were getting on and that at midnight, everyone went home safely. A retired garda, Mick Hanrahan, who lived in Loughbollard, became a great friend to us all. He enthralled us with various stories of his time in the gardaí right from 1922 onwards. He proudly would show us his tunic and baton which he said he used as often as required. He had a fantastic grasp of international affairs and predicted that China was the country to watch for the future. Time will vindicate his prediction.

These are memories firmly imprinted, never to be forgotten and that is the value of life – nobody can ever take away our recollections of the past.

Growing up in Clane in the Sixties *Mary McManmon*

I am one of sixteen in our family. At mealtimes, my mum would put a pot of stew in the middle of the table and we all tucked in. We had no fancy dishes. Mum and Dad worked so hard for us. My dad was a great fisherman. We are a great family – thanks to our parents. They were fantastic.

Mary Timpson (McManmon)

Members of the family – Nelly, Tom, Paddy, Peter, Mary, Bernie, Seán, Noel, Tony, Stan, Patricia, Anne, Paschal, Claude, Margaret and Vera.

Mary McManmon.

Paddy and Mrs McManmon.

Seán McManmon with Salmon prize.

Clane: the village we knew

BOTTOM RIGHT—The four Cash brothers who rode in the Open Maiden race for the O'Dwyer Memorial Trophy at the Sth. Co. Dublin point-to-point. Left to right — Jas. Cash (who was second), E. Cash, M. Cash and John Cash (who rode the winner Swell Party).

The four Cash brothers who rode in the Open Maiden race for the O'Dwyer Memorial Trophy at the Sth. Co. Dublin point-to-point. Left to right – J. Cash (who was second), E. Cash, M. Cash and John Cash (who rode the winner Swell Party).

XXII

HORSES ARE MY LIFE – NED CASH

Des Maguire

Reproduced with kind permission of the *Irish Farmers Journal* from the book *Horses are my Life* by Des Maguire.

As tractors took over from the working horse and cars began to completely replace ponies on the roads, I started to buy a better class of horse suitable for Hunting, Point-to-Points and Racing.

The development of mechanisation had a devastating impact on the traditional horse fairs. Many of them disappeared altogether and with them went hundreds of small dealers whose bread and butter depended on buying and selling them. There emerged however a more specialist type of dealer capable of adapting to changed market requirements and who was prepared to go around to farms and assemble horses suitable for the leisure trade. I made the transition without any difficulty.

I started to buy hunters and showjumpers in big numbers for people like Mark Chambers in England, Frank and Joe Kiernan and Jim Maguire in the north, and Joe McGrath whose demand was more for racehorses. Orders poured in from people who wanted me to buy a good horse for them and there was no shortage of breeders and farmers who wanted me to call to inspect horses they were trying to sell

I got interested in Point-to-Pointing myself and encouraged all my children to ride. Ned Junior who later became one of the country's top showjumpers representing Ireland twice on Aga Khan teams, started off with me at Point-to-Points, so did my daughter Margaret who jumped for Ireland's Junior team at one stage and my son Jim was only fourteen years of age when he won one of the top races at Punchestown with a horse called You Mind Me.

I remember when I bought this horse he hadn't got a name and I was out in the yard with Jim, rubbing down the animal when I heard him saying to the horse 'Won't you mind me now?' I had promised to let Jim ride him in a Point-to-Point the following week. 'What are you going to call him'? He asked. 'You've named him', I said. 'You Mind Me is as good a name as any'. Jim won several Point-to-Points on 'You Mind Me' and after he won at Punchestown I sold him.

I had a few other good Point-to-Pointers like Donnelly's Joy, Chimney Smoke and Misty Hope all of which had the distinction of winning two races on the one day. I bought Chimney Smoke from Teddy Coonan. Pat Hogan, a former Minister for Agriculture had him once. He was a good racehorse but hadn't got the best of legs. We hunted him and hardened up his legs and he never gave a lame step with us. We sold all these horses after we had won Point-to-Points with them.

I sold a very good racehorse to Joe McGrath called Vulissimo. Before I bought him he was owned by the Dublin hotelier John Costello who had a stud farm outside Maynooth and he was trained by Ned Callaghan. The first time they ran the horse he was fourth in a very good bumper and they could have got a lot of money for him but wouldn't sell. Next time out the horse ran badly and his performance in subsequent races grew gradually worse. Ned Callaghan thought he might be having heart trouble and called in a vet who told him that in his opinion the horse had a trace of a murmur in his heart. Ned and John Costello decided to sell anyway and I was asked whether I would be interested in buying the animal. Ned Callaghan told me that the horse had a murmur in his heart and their asking price was £200. I paid for the animal – a very good-looking four-year-old – brought him home, and turned him out to grass for three months. Then I brought him back in and started to hunt him.

I ran him in a Point-to-Point at Fairyhouse with my son Mick aboard and he looked as if he was going to be well beaten coming up to four fences from home. Then two riders cornered Mick and tried to down him at the fourth-last fence. Mick got vexed, hit the horse a couple of belts with his stick and Vulissimo went on to win by six lengths. Mick told me afterwards he was going to pull up the horse after the fourth-last because he had dropped the bit. The following week we brought the horse to Wexford and the same thing happened. He dropped the bit again about four fences from home, Mick belted him with the stick again and he went on to win by about ten lengths. Joe McGrath was watching and came over to me after the race. 'That's a very decent sort of horse', he said. 'He is', I agreed. 'How much do you want for him'? 'I'll take £2,000'. 'Right', said Joe.

Before we clinched the deal I told Joe that before I bought the horse he was supposed to have a bad heart, so he better have him checked out by a vet. Joe's vet found no trace of a murmur so he gave me my £2,000 which was ten times more than I originally paid for him. Joe ran the horse in a hurdle, but he hit a hurdle and he wouldn't go on. He came over to my place and said 'That horse is a right dodger'. 'What's wrong with him?' 'He laid down on the jockey about four fences from home'. 'There's nothing wrong with the horse', I said. 'You enter him in a Point-to-Point, get Mick to ride him, be there when he's running and put the glasses on him about four fences from home. I bet you you'll see the horse hacking, the next thing he'll drop the bit and make sure you watch him after that'.

Joe McGrath entered him in a Point-to-Point at Punchestown. Pat Hogan had a very good horse running in the same race and his connections were saying he couldn't be beaten. Vulissimo acted up as usual four fences from home but Mick spurred him on with his stick and they beat Pat Hogan's good horse. Joe McGrath was satisfied. Vulissimo then went on to win a lot of good races including the Leopardstown Chase. Later Joe was offered a lot of money for him and he went to England where he won a number of good races before breaking a leg.

I was never a great man for going to the races and when I do; my normal bet is only £10. The only horse of my own I ever had a sizeable bet on was Master Ken, a well-bred horse by Master Buck which belonged to Ken Urquhart, with whom I used to hunt. His widow put him up for sale in the RDS as a three-year-old, just broken, and I bought him for £750.

Liam Brennan, the trainer, was always on to me to buy a horse that he could train for me and I gave him Master Ken which I named him after my late friend. He won hurdle races in

Killarney and Galway and I had £100 on him each time. He was returned at 4/1 in Killarney and 3/1 in Galway. He didn't do much after that and I eventually sold him to my son Jim for around £3,000.

I've been to nine or ten Aintree Grand Nationals in my time but the one I remember best was the 1964 Grand National in which a horse I bought for Jack Prendergast of Kilcock, Valouis, ran.

I tried to sell Valouis behind Jack's back to an Englishman after the race for a bit of crack. I bought Valouis from a farmer outside Edgeworthstown who had told me several times that he would like to sell me a horse for one of my sons, Jim or Ned to ride. He rang me one night and told me he was bringing a horse to the Dublin sales which he thought would suit one of the boys. I went up to the sales but the horse wasn't there so I drove on to Edgeworthstown to see what had gone wrong.

'You hadn't the horse at the sales', I said to the farmer.

'No, he was turned down yesterday. He had a curve on him,' he replied.

'I'm very disappointed because I was expecting a good bit of money for him'.

Now I had never seen the animal but I knew that the farmer was a very decent fellow so I said to him: 'Curve and all, how much do you want for him?'

'I'd sell him for £200', he said.

'I'll buy him'.

'There's one condition', the farmer said. 'I want you to call the horse Valouis. He is by Richard Louis out of a mare called Val Air and I would like him to be called Valouis so that I will recognise him if he ever does get a race'.

'No problem'.

I rang Jack Prendergast who was a good friend of mine and who was always on the lookout for a good bargain and told him that I had bought a racehorse which would suit him.

'How much do you want for him?'

'I want £350'.

'I'll give you £300 and I'll pay you for him immediately'.

Valouis went on to win eight good races in Ireland and he also won the Molyneaux Chase in Liverpool. I am convinced that he would also have won the 1964 Grand National only for the fact that he was brought down at Beechers, the second time round.

I went over on the boat to see him run, paid into the course, and conned my way into the Grand Stand and the Owners and Trainers Bar by flashing a Punchestown ticket that I had around my glasses at the men in the white coats. I met several people I knew in the bar, and one of them Donie Howard, a horse dealer invited me to lunch with some of his friends in a box in the Grand Stand. One of these was a very wealthy man who bred trotting horses. I got talking to him and told him I had come over from Ireland just to back Valouis. 'Do you own him? 'I do'. Valouis ran a great race before being brought down at Beechers. I had a fiver on him.

Later in the evening Donie Howard's friend asked me if I would sell Valouis to him. I was well on and started to deal with him, even though Valouis wasn't mine to sell. I agreed to swap him Valouis for a good trotting mare and £1,000. 'There's one condition', I said. 'The horse got a cut when he fell at Beechers. We'll have a look at him in the morning and if he is alright we'll do the deal'.

I went back into Liverpool and had a good few drinks before rushing to catch the boat home. Naturally I never showed up the following morning. When I got back to Clane I told Jack Prendergast that I had tried to swap Valouis for a trotting mare and £1,000. 'I wouldn't have taken £20,000 for him', Jack said but he enjoyed the story. I ran into Donie Howard about a month later and he chided me for not turning up to finalise the deal. 'That man was there the following morning with the readies to pay you and he was going to give me £100 for making the introductions', Donie said.

My performance was so good that even Donie, a horse dealer himself, didn't know that I was having them on.

I MEET THE QUEEN MOTHER

I have bought and sold thousands of horses in my sixty years of active dealing and several internationally known horses have passed through my hands.

The best-known of these are Look Out which was the top national showjumper in Ireland during the mid-seventies; Condy, which is still one of the best horses in Ireland today; Carousel which I sold to the army and which, when renamed Castlepark, proved to be one of the fastest speed horses on the Continent; Dun Gleen, which represented Ireland twice on Aga Khan teams; and Derrypatrick, which was one of the most valuable horses to come my way.

But I also bought and sold several other top class horses including Mostrim, Lydican, Thatch (Inis Mhor), Sliabh na mBan, Buttevant Boy, Moydrum, Slaney, Wellington, Nordell, Bandalero, Daddy's Girl, Hopeful Marcus, Cool Bawn, Andante, Thor, Doneraile, Snaffles and Mr Spock, to name but a few.

Some of the best-known personalities in showjumping have ridden my horses, Eddie Macken, Con Power, Paul Darragh, James Kernan, Michael Hickey, Seamus Hayes, Billy Ringrose, Seamus Brennan, Larry Kiely, Gerry Mullins, Graham Fletcher, Marian Coakes, Ted Edgar, Johnny Greenwood, Cecil Mahon, George Stewart, my sons Ned Junior and Michael and my grandson, Michael Walsh, who is now carrying on the family tradition.

For the past twelve years I have been represented at the Aga Khan by a horse I put through my hands at one stage or another and there isn't a major competition in Ireland that a horse of mine hasn't won.

My own personal favourite was Look Out which was the leading national horse in Ireland for four seasons. Ned Junior won the Spillers Bursary several years running on him. The horse represented Ireland on a winning Nations Cup team in 1973 and won major competitions in Geneva and Rome.

Con Power won a Derby Trial and seven international classes with him. Look Out was selected for the 1974 Aga Khan team but picked up a virus and had to be replaced by Dun Gleen another one of my horses. I bought the horse from Frank Fitzgerald of Leggestratt House, Kilkenny, who has produced a lot of top-quality showjumpers and kept him for four very successful seasons during which Ned Junior represented Ireland twice on Aga Khan teams.

Ned Cash receiving his winner's trophy for his horse at Ward Union point-to-point.

I was delighted that Ned Junior had so much success. Indeed, when he was at the height of his success in the mid-seventies I was even introduced to Britain's Queen Mother as Ned Cash Junior's father. It happened when Ned had won a competition at the Royal Show in Stoneleigh and was presented to the Queen Mother in the Royal Box afterwards.

'Who did you come over with Mr Cash?' she asked him.

'My father, ma'am', he replied.

'Well as this is a family day bring him up to the Royal Box so I can meet him' she said.

I was presented to the Queen Mother, a charming person, and she said she hoped that I would enjoy myself on the town later that night.

'Sorry I can't take you with me ma'am, I'm booked up for the night, but if you ever want a good horse be sure to look me up in Ireland', I told her.

She smiled as we made our way back down the stand. She had a good sense of humour.

XXIII

THE FINAL CHAPTER IN THE HISTORY OF THE OLD BOYS' SCHOOL

Pat Lynch

'Do you stock white football socks?' the customer asked. 'Certainly' replied the shopkeeper producing a lily-white pair suitable for a gentleman. 'I need twenty-one pairs, not so large'. 'Serious? Are these for boys or for men?' the shopkeeper inquired. 'They are for the men of tomorrow'. 'Look, let's get this straight' he said, 'Is the game being played today or tomorrow?' 'This evening at 6.30p.m.'. Deal done.

That was in the mid-sixties. Since then four decades of life have crept stealthily by. Tomorrow has arrived. The boys from the old boys' school on the Dublin road have grown into men, enjoying the good experiences of life, shouldering life's varied burdens. A young man in his twenties comes dangerously close to the entrance of the twilight zone. A clock may stop ticking but time marches on.

The old boys' school, built in 1839, refurbished in 1929 and again in 1963, consisted of three classrooms. There were seventy-five pupils on roll. Like several other schools throughout rural Ireland, conditions were antiquated. A number of families passed by in search of better conditions, a better foundation for the life ahead. Most returned later. Others sought admission from adjoining parishes. The girls who received First Holy Communion were served breakfast in the convent while the boys dined at the teacher's house on the Dublin Road.

The teaching staff consisted of Dublin man Pat Dempsey and Ms Mary Burke from Galway. A third teacher arrived. Very soon he purchased a new car: not a Mercedes or a BMW, not a Ford Escort or a Prefect, nor a Corsair, but a Mini Minor. A tallish man, some wondered how he fitted into it! The purchase price in the town of Tralee was £460. Barney will still tell you the number plate reading. This modest automobile would complete the 200-mile journey from Kildare to Kerry for the princely sum of £1 – petrol costing 5s per gallon. Take-home pay was £11 10s per week, or £600 per annum. Full board, breakfast, packed lunch, dinner and evening tea cost £4 per week.

Four cows grazed the school field, now the property of Clane Lawn Tennis Club. It was out of bounds for the boys' football games, not allowed. At 12.35p.m. on Monday 9 May 1966 a boy re-entered the classroom at lunch break. 'Can we play football sir'? The cheer, which greeted him from the assembled group outside the main door, heralded the end for the four harmless animals. They would have to move on. The boy now runs his own business sitting high on a lorry, worth in excess of £100,000. He passes through Clane at 6.45a.m. most mornings. He always salutes. That year the farmers of Ireland walked to Leinster House in search of the Minister for Agriculture, Charlie Haughey.

A primary inter-schools league in the Parish of Clane was won by Clane in 1966. Seán Cribbin had been playing a major roll organising the boys. 'Put your hearts into it lads', he would say. Towering full-back John O'Brien from Blackhall was said to have a great future. Peter O'Neill of Credit Union fame acted the part of the original bomber at No.14. P.J. Wallace was there, cool under pressure, Ger Corrigan too and Peter Burke. Peadar McCormack, later a Cheltenham jockey and Irish Grand National jockey, and Billy King, destined for building contracting as well as Liam Ross whose family owned the farm on which Clonwood Heights now stands. All sixth class boys at that time were fourteen years of age. Sister Perpetua's secondary school was not yet ready to open for boys. This would happen a year later. Five girls sat the school's first Leaving Cert in 1968. Ask Ann Noonan or Liz Higgins. The boys mentioned earlier left Clane school on 30 June 1966. Some attended Naas CBS and others went to work.

The year of 1967 was a great year for the school. Serious work needed to be undertaken within the classroom, serious games were played. It was the last year of the Primary Certificate Examination for sixth classes throughout Ireland. The Clane boys were happy with their results. The boys retained the Parish Cup. A fabulous parish schoolboy team won the football league for County Kildare's Rural Schools and subsequently defeated the Urban winners by a twelve-point margin in the Division One final proper. Eight games were played. Only one goal passed reliable full-back Billy Graham and goalkeeper John Gill from Timahoe – a record for schoolboy football. Lar Casey was resolute at number two as was wing-back Michael Holligan, now an engineer with Kildare County Council. Billy Moloney, who cycled to school, right hand in pocket, left hand steering the bicycle, presently a nurse in far-away Oz, partnered Paddy Browne at midfield. The jinking Cooney brothers Joe, resident of the New Road, Straffan and Seamie, block-layer during the construction of the two new schools in 1981/82, and now doing same in Australia, were both a treat to watch. Ambrose Bracken, Des Behan, Jack Graham, Pat Cribbin, Richardstown, Brendan Mahony and Denis Holligan all played a part. Paul Smullen of McCabe and Smullen wore the number twelve. Big Willie Sullivan from Coill Dubh scored 3-5 in the first game against Rathangan.

Later that year the teacher announced, 'We will have a sports day on the Friday of next week'. 'What are sports?' one boy asked. Televisions were still exceptionally rare in homes, there were only perhaps two or three. A tall gangly boy from fifth standard cleared 4ft 3in in the high jump – no practice, no western roll, no scissors kick, simply up and over! He still holds that record, I presume. His name was Jim. He is taller now.

In 1968, the recent GAA chairman, Declan Corrigan, wearing number six, led Clane to an Under-12 county title, division 1. He was ably assisted by Barney McCormack (number two) Peter McIntyre who later on, like Barney and Declan, became Senior County Champion, left-footed Colm Behan wearing number four, the Behan brothers, Edmond and Brian and Declan Mahony of Q & M. The tall Blackhall duo, John Daly of Clane Steel Garden Sheds fame, and restaurateur Tommy Hoban, now resident in London, both manned the midfield positions. John Noonan was there to steady the ship, as was Christy Walsh of Digby Bridge, Ger Langan, Pascal McManmon, John Cribbin, Castlebrowne, Harry Bracken and Kevin Byrne who played in goals. Wing-back J.P. Holligan wrote the winning account of that match thirty-eight years ago!

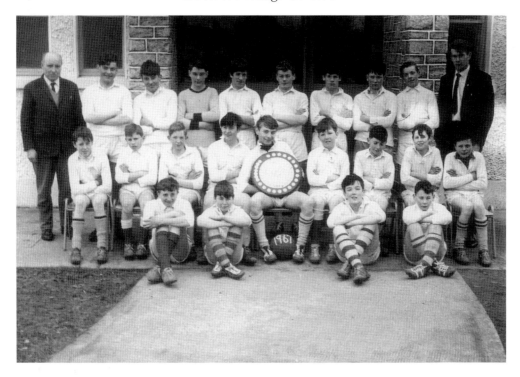

The Clane Under-14s, 1967. Back row: S. Cribbin, T. Kenny, L. Casey, J. Gill, P. Browne, B. Graham, D. Behan, B. Moloney, B. Mahony, P. Lynch. Second row: J. Cooney, L. Murphy, P. Smullen, M. Byrne, D. Fox (captain), M. Holligan, A. Bracken, S. Cooney, P. Cribbin. Front row: P.J. Carew, M. Murphy, D. Holligan, J. Graham.

Basketball leagues were introduced. The games were played on an L-shaped area of concrete at the rear of the school – the world's first L-shaped basketball court! The uprights were embedded in two half-tar barrels and fastened to the roofs of the two open sheds. Table tennis was introduced.

All boys from third to sixth classes took part in all football and basketball leagues. Medals were awarded to the winners and the runners-up for the first time. How they were appreciated.

In the classrooms heating was dependent on three tall turf stoves, which seldom functioned properly. The turf was supplied by Jack Brennan from Coill Dubh. He wore a heavy black overcoat and black beret, and loved to engage in the art of conversation. Ms Emily O'Rourke, who cleaned the three rooms and set the fires for the morning, was an honourable lady. Her wages amounted to £1.10.00d. per week. She worked at the school for one hour a day. The fires were ignited at 8.30a.m., but generally by 8.45a.m. they had given up the struggle. This necessitated re-kindling in the hope that some heat would materialise by 11.00a.m. Boys and teachers got on with the work. Everybody survived. Insulation had not arrived. Caretakers, secretaries, parent associations and boards of management belonged to the future.

Joan Ryan, later Mrs Leacy, arrived from Tralee to join the staff in 1969. Later on, as numbers grew, she would find herself educating four classes consisting of fifty-two children in Junior Infants, Senior Infants, First and Second Classes. She later became vice-principal, a post she still holds in Scoil Phádraig.

The school hoped to lay the foundations for all types of future careers. The games always helped to create a good attitude towards work and positive endeavour. If it's worth doing, it's worth doing well. The name of the job is not the most important thing as every person has an important part to play.

The sixties passed with a front-page headline in the *Leinster Leader*: 'A million pound project for Clane'. Disbelief? The Connolly brothers from County Mayo were about to begin a development in Manzor's field - once the home of Clane GAA Club, on the Kilcock road. The only estate in Clane at that time, apart from the row of beautiful old-style homes on the Naas road, was St Brigid's Terrace, which consisted of twelve houses. Loughbollard estate sprung into existence. The Feely family from Dublin were the first occupants – house No.4, currently the home of Joe and Clare McDonald and family. The cost of a house was £3,050. On a July morning in 1969 at around 3.00a.m., as 1,000 young people danced in the marquee at Clane GAA carnival, Neil Armstrong set foot on the moon: 'One small step for a man, one giant leap for mankind', he uttered. The creation of Loughbollard was, in its own way, a giant leap for Clane – the first of many leaps. Clane is still leaping!

The sixties passed. The seventies arrived. Playground space at the old boys' school on the Dublin road got more confined as each year a new prefab needed to be provided, totalling seven extra rooms and finally a caravan to be used as a classroom. There were now a total of eleven classrooms. Heads collided regularly in the small play space, necessitating the attention of the local doctors Rynne and Flanagan.

Over the years, literally hundreds of boys achieved a very high standard in the skills of Gaelic football. The children all enjoyed their games – a most important consideration. Internal school leagues would give each individual an opportunity to win a place on the various school teams. The positive work ethic of the school was built around participation in games, ensuring children's happiness and personal satisfaction. This brought about the realisation that with committed effort, on and off the field of play, personal success and well-being is always possible.

Many boys from this era would emerge to wear the white jersey of Clane and Kildare in the various grades of Minor, under-21 and Senior. Billy Moloney, Declan Corrigan, Peter McIntyre, Seamie Cooney, Ambrose Bracken, Lar Higgins, Harry Bracken, Barney McCormack and John Cribbin would win Senior County Championships with Clane. Billy Graham would lead Raheens to a Leinster Club title while his brother Jack would captain Kildare to a Leinster Minor title. Later Matthew Behan, Frank Mahony, Peter McCreery, Pat Cribbin, John Cribbin, Chris Merriman, Ed Daly, Danny Horan and others would emerge to win under-16 back-to-back County Championships for Clane under the stewardship of Frank McLoughlin.

Towards the end of the sixties another group of 'babes' were just about entering the world or learning to walk or crawl at different locations! The three O'Connell brothers were finding their feet in Boston and Micheal Conneff was coming to terms with the many new and exciting experiences of life on the farm at Kilmurry. Brian Connolly, Willie McCreery, Tom Keane, Kevin Murphy, David Cummins, Adrian Power, David Delaney, Harry Ryan, Des King, Mick and Tommy Smith, Oscar Shortt, Ray Kelly, Seamus McCarthy Paul McLoughlin, the Nugents, Seán Boland, Mick Boland, Johnny O'Shea of Baltreacy, Jim Callan, the Dorans, Paul and John Heneghan, Ger Lyons, the Dunnes, Paul McDonald, would all join to form fabulous schoolboy teams. They would later contest two county minor finals under manager Barney McCormack. Quite a few would win senior championships with Clane. Paul McLoughlin would wear the Kildare jersey from the age of eighteen onwards. So too would Willie and Denis O'Connell at a later date. Paul would travel from Fermoy three times a week to train with Kildare in Newbridge. This was one of the best groups of players ever to represent the school.

Other groups would follow, learning the basic skills at the old boys' school. Four would win All-Ireland 'B' Colleges – Martin Lynch, John Finn, Kevin McDonald, Tom Sullivan – and represent Kildare in various grades at a later stage. Two would be honoured by the All-Star Selection Committee at National level – Martin Lynch and John Finn. Other contemporaries of that era who showed outstanding football ability at primary school level were Ronan King, Niall Murphy, Dan and Christy O'Shea, Mike Buckley, John Cribbin, Niall and Shane McCorley, Jimmy Boland, John Gartland, Dermot Coonan – all quality players. With better playing facilities in the new school, Scoil Phádraig, which opened in 1982, would contest a total of fifty-eight finals over an eighteen-year period up to the year 2000. One group would win All-Ireland Féile. Eddie and Paul McCormack would grace Croke Park as would Domo Cribbin. Several would win Minor and Senior County Championships with Clane.

While over twenty teachers serving for various periods of time on the staff at the old boys' school from the mid-sixties onwards, each helping to build up the school's standard, some gave long years of commitment. These include Nora O'Connor, Patsy O'Riordan, Teresa Grace, Maureen McCormack and Ciarán McCarthy, in addition to Joan Leacy, who has already been mentioned. Pat Costello arrived from Galway for the final year of the school's existence in 1981, liked what he saw, and stayed on to eventually become principal of the new Scoil Phádraig, eighteen years later.

On a June day in 1982 throngs of local residents lined the village street as 360 pupils from each of the old schools – boys and girls – marched to the lovely new schools on the Prosperous road. A new era had dawned. More comfortable times lay ahead but fabulous experiences from the old days would not be forgotten. Our yesterdays can never be left behind. They are part of what we have become. It is always a pleasure to meet the boys of yesterday, the builders, the mechanics, the gardaí, the electricians, the teachers, the pilots, the accountants, the carpenters, the drivers, the self-employed, the landscapers, the plasterers, the painters, and the jockeys to reminisce about by-gone days. One hopes they are happy as they traverse the road of life. To the parents who afforded us the honour and the responsibility of knowing what is dearest to them – their children - and helping to educate them over a thirty-five-year period, we say it was our privilege and joy.

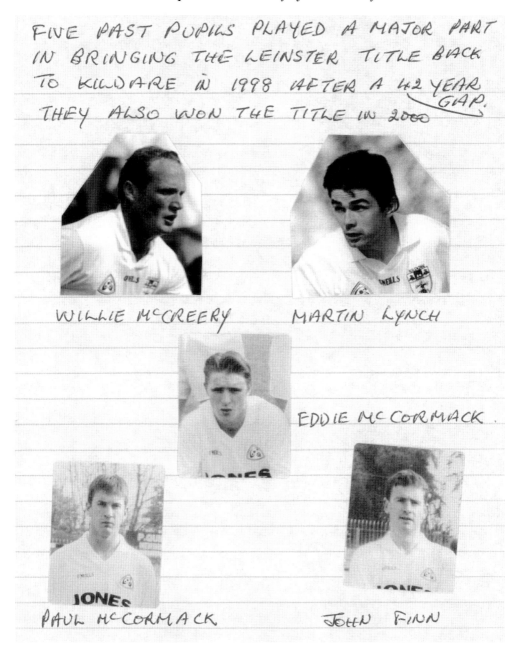

FIVE PAST PUPILS PLAYED A MAJOR PART
IN BRINGING THE LEINSTER TITLE BACK
TO KILDARE IN 1998 AFTER A 42 YEAR
THEY ALSO WON THE TITLE IN 2000 GAP.

WILLIE McCREERY   MARTIN LYNCH

EDDIE McCORMACK.

PAUL McCORMACK   JOHN FINN

Five past pupils played a major part in bringing the Leinster title back to Kildare in 1998 after a forty-two-year gap. They also won the title in 2000. Top left: Willie McCreery, top right: Martin Lynch, middle: Eddie McCormack, bottom left: Paul McCormack, bottom right: John Finn.

XXIV

REMEMBERING THE VILLAGE STREET OF THE SIXTIES

Pat Lynch

Water flowed gently underneath the Liffey Bridge on the Naas road, continuing on its meandering journey from the serenity of the Wicklow mountains to Dublin Bay, there to be engulfed by the waters of the Irish Sea. Today water still flows under the bridge; not the same water – the same bridge, the same Clane – if only in name. Life is somewhat similar. People have passed by on life's journey. Others have come. Is it not people that make a place, a town, a village? People change a village.

The Corner House is still there. Formerly it was Geoghegans, later Carroll's and then Dillons. Jones' and Manzor's are there, though both have experienced life-shattering transformations. Behan's grocery shop at the Naas end of the village street bears the name Dave's. Connolly's at the other end also has a new owner. The little thatched shop where Bridie and Eileen worked has long since crumbled before the bulldozer to be replaced by one of the new inventions – the supermarket – called Londis. The commercial life of Clane at one time consisted of three grocery shops, three pubs, a post office, a chemist and a barber's shop, with all other buildings being residential. John and Mrs McKenna ran a grocery and general store on the Dublin road leading out of Clane Village.

Georgie Dunn's home and post office have disappeared, along with the horses in the backyard, where the O' Neill family once sold milk. They have made way for Peony Palace, AIB, a barbers shop, a bookmaker, Zest, and an underground car park, which was never heard of in the Clane of the sixties. Old shops which had already closed for business by the mid-sixties, such as McEvoys and Dalys, have been reinvented as Marie's Antiques, and Manzor's Gift and Stationery Store respectively. Jim Malone's homely barber shop has been dressed in a lovely new outfit.

The old garda barracks of the sixties later became the home of the Merriman family. In more recent times Pat and Sheila Walsh sold fresh fruit and vegetables in part of this historic landmark. One can purchase a bracelet, an engagement ring, or a watch from the jeweller that occupies another part of the building. Sgt Liam Egan now enjoys the quiet life in a peaceful, rural setting, among the fields and the bogs, the trees and the birds, alerted by the intermittent bark of a dog or a far-away fox.

Doyles' family home, recently the location of Clane post office has become Mrs Quin's. It also housed another modern development called a bistro. Next door the home of the Shortt family is the setting for McCormack's Auctioneers and Insurance as well as another first for Clane – Given's Opticians. College Cabs salute us from the upper level. They have replaced the Rowan Tree of more recent times.

Tom McEvoy and Peig O'Reilly outside
the church, with Jimmy Dunne in the
background.

The old Handball Alley has given way to Tom Gough's butcher shop and Clane Business School. Peter Wallace's bicycle repair shop has been transformed into P. J. Trophy and Cycles Store. Here John Delaney follows in the footsteps of his postman uncle and repair specialist Paddy Delaney. Further down the street the Collins family home houses Macari's Italian Take Away and Mario's Pizza & Pasta as well as Bobb's Hair Salon.

Whatever happened to Byrne's butcher shop, that stately two-storey house, opposite the church gate? It once housed a tiny version of the bank in the days of one desk and two chairs. Here men sat to chat on the three steps before and after Mass on Sundays. Today the only steps are indoors in a new building. They lead to Yvonne's Playworld – a playschool on the first floor and to Mags' Hair Salon. A playschool? Children in the sixties played on the street, in back gardens and in fields.

Was it not on the street, or more precisely in the entrance between the family home and the convent that Lord Mayor Dessie learned the art of goalkeeping? Later he would defend for Clane, for Kildare and for Leinster. The pharmacy, owned by the same Dessie, has grown from a one-room unit to encompass the entire house and beyond, where his dad, Sgt Peter Marron, reared pigs and calves in his backyard, now Marron Court, home to several industries.

Larkin's Butcher Stall, which operated at Manzor's Corner since 1961, later moved to a new location at Byrne's, where the proprietor, Tom, had himself previously run a small butcher stall. Following the retirement of Pat, the ground floor is now occupied by Bambury's Bookmakers and Q & M Drapery Store. Dr Flanagan's family home, once the home of the Geoghegans, the O'Malleys, the Walsh family, the Daltons and originally the Cartons, clings proudly to its former character.

Father Doyle's grave.

The Ulster Bank has found a home in Clane. Doctors, dentists, accountants, solicitors, and travel agents have all also taken up residence in Clane. Did we have Chinese restaurants, bistros or pizzerias in the Clane of the sixties? Occasions and Attitude are new, as are perfumeries and beauticians, florists, chiropodists and Montessori schools. What was wrong with our vision in the sixties? Now we have Xtra-Vision!

Boutiques were unheard of then. Clothes, formerly washed in homes and hung out to dry are now dried indoors, since the arrival of Bracken's Sparkleen, also occupying part of McEvoys. Beyond the Liffey bridge, Clane's football jerseys were a regular sight hanging in the breeze to dry, having been washed by the Gorman family under the watchful eye of Joe 'France' Bracken. Larry Slevin remembers the day when only four cars were parked in Clane.

Mobile phone owners of today may not be aware that in the mid-sixties there were only five house phones in Clane, and perhaps fewer than five TVs. Fridges were just about arriving, and dishwashers and washing machines were either very rare or things of the future. Most physical outdoor work was still done by pick, spade and shovel, although the tractor had made its way on to farms. Bulldozers were just making an appearance.

In the mid-sixties the Parish Priest's cows still sauntered lazily through the village street, under the watchful eye of Seán Cullen from Millicent Cross. They were making their way home from the pastures on the Prosperous road, where Aldi now functions.

For Father John Doyle PP, like so many others, time has marched on. He lies at rest in the churchyard. His grave, until recently, bore the inscription 'Kneel and Pray'. Few seem to kneel, but perhaps many offer a prayer in passing.

Charlie's and Cash's horses added an extra spectacle to the village street as they passed by. So too did herds of cattle being herded along by Pat Shortt and Joe Higgins. Rush times and traffic jams had not yet come to Clane.

In keeping with a very old rural Irish tradition, men assembled to chat after Mass outside the church gate – the farmers on the right, the sports lovers on the left. Farmers discussed progress on the farm, the hay, the turf, the weather, the price of a good cow, a calf, a horse, the condition of the corn or the price for this year.

The footballers wondered how Clane would do today against Raheens or Carbury. Didn't Pa have a tremendous game last Sunday for Kildare, taking them out of the clouds and driving them seventy or eighty yards, the young garda with the great pair of hands who had arrived having played with his county Under-21s , the young curate, the makings of a future long-kick champion. Any tips for Punchestown, Naas or Fairyhouse? Did McCreery have any winners at Downroyal?

Veteran Dinny Colgan cycled into Clane on an old straight-handle-bar bicycle. So too did Patsy Gorman, Johnny Nevin and Mick Archer. Joe Bracken, Seán Cribbin, Tom Merriman, Jim Daly, Paddy McCormack and others worked tirelessly on behalf of the GAA club. The ICA was one of the very few other organisations apart from the table tennis club.

Standing stately in the background was the Presentation Convent, just as it does today. At the time the nuns had lived among the people of Clane for over one hundred years. They had made a massive contribution to the field of education at a time when these services were not readily available. Their contribution was voluntary. They never received personal pay for their labours. Today they have said their goodbyes to the people of Clane and to the village that they loved. Their work should be appreciated and remembered. The nuns sourced the sites on which the three new schools stand.

During those years the local GAA club deserved special appreciation. Over a period of seven weeks every summer, the members, male and female, devoted themselves to raising the funds for the development of Conneff Park, which would become the club's permanent home. This necessitated long hours of work, day and night, planning and organising field days, pony races, donkey derbies, football tournaments, poker classics and especially marquee dances. Large tents were erected. Dancing floors were laid. Bands were organised, as were doormen, stewards, ticket sellers and others. The members of the Ladies' Committee served tea, sandwiches and minerals until 3.00a.m., three nights a week. Voluntary workers went home at 4.00a.m. on Saturday nights and returned at 8.00a.m. to prepare for Sunday's activities. A percentage of the proceeds was always donated to the Presentation Sisters for the fledgling post-primary school. Seldom was such a demonstration of voluntary effort in a community witnessed.

The parish of Clane and Rathcoffey included Staplestown, Timahoe and Coill Dubh at that time. The parish priest resided in the Old Presbytery, while three curates shared a house on the Prosperous road. This is the house immediately beyond the site of the three-storey apartments that are presently being constructed in the original convent field, site of Aldi. Almost everybody attended Mass on Sundays, taking the Lord at His word: 'Do this in memory of me'.

Father Edward Flood

The opening of Father Bob Thompson Business Park, Clane.

EPILOGUE

A picture is a thousand words: we hope that the photos and text of this book have given you the opportunity to look through the window at a particular time to view the fabric of society in Clane from 1945 onwards. People and events make our lives more colourful and brighten the mundane schedule of daily life with humour.

Cardinal Newman said 'To live is to change and to change is to live'. This certainly has been the case in our beloved village. Progress cannot be stopped – it is like King Canute attempting to prevent the waves of the sea coming to the shore. Progress can be so accelerated that it is difficult to cope with on occasions.

We feel honoured and privileged to have had our childhood in the era of the fifties and sixties – so much so that it has motivated us to write this book – *Clane: The Village We Knew*.

Paddy Behan
Liam Burke
Bryan Sammon